# HOW TO DO
# Science Experiments
# WITH CHILDREN

By Joan Bentley and Linda Hobbs

Congratulations on your purchase of some of the finest teaching materials in the world.

**Authors: Joan Bentley and Linda Hobbs**
**Editor: Jo Ellen Moore**
**Illustrator: Joy Evans**

Entire contents of compiled version copyright ©1994
by EVAN-MOOR CORP.
18 Lower Ragsdale Drive, Monterey, CA 93940-5746

Original editions:
*Science Experiments Volume 1*, © 1991 by Evan-Moor Corp.
*Science Experiments Volume 2*, © 1991 by Evan-Moor Corp.
*Science Experiments Volume 3*, © 1991 by Evan-Moor Corp.

# How to Do Science Experiments with Children

These experiments have been successfully used in first through third grades. One experiment was done each week. Although each lesson was demonstrated by the teacher as students observed, many of the experiments can be done successfully by second and third graders working in pairs or small groups with adult guidance for a "hands-on" experience.

General directions for conducting any of the experiments with your class are given on page 7.

Specific directions for each of the seventy experiments contain:

- a teacher information page explaining what is to be done and the expected result.
- a scientific method sheet providing a place for children to record information and directions on how to do the experiment.
- reproducible pictures for predicting outcome of the experiment.

Two parent letters are provided. The first letter explains what is happening in your science program at school. The second letter requests parents to send items to be used in the experiments.

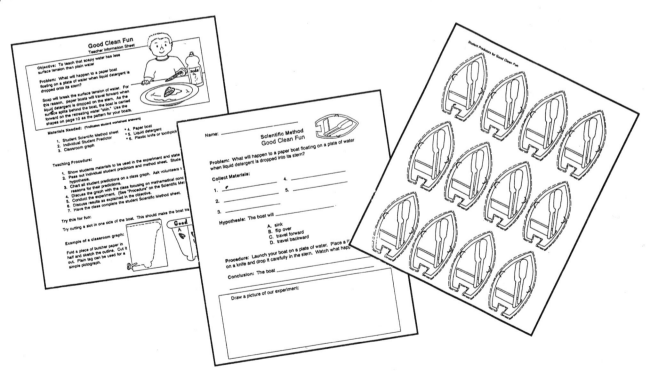

# Table of Contents

## Sound

## Static Electricity

## Forces

### • Action and Reaction

### • Inertia and Momentum

### • Adhesion and Cohesion

### • Pressure

### • Gravity

## Parent Letters

How to Do Experiments with Children

# Getting Ready

## Before You Begin

Before starting any experiment, follow these simple steps:

- Read both the Teacher Information page and the Scientific Method sheet.
- Collect the materials you need to conduct the experiment.
- Try out the experiment to familiarize yourself with the procedures and expected results.
- Prepare the graph form and reproduce copies of the predictors.

## Helpful Hints

Teachers are sometimes hesitant to do experiments because of the mess. Before beginning any experiment, think about the area in which you will be working, the materials you will be using, and how you can keep the mess to a minimum. Here are some tips that have worked for us:

- Work on a tray or shallow plastic tub. This will catch spills and overflows.
- Keep plenty of paper towels handy for hands and for spills when they do occur.
- If the experiment is one involving popping corks or hot water, tape off an "out-of-bounds" area showing where children many not walk or stand during the experiment.
- Emphasis safety frequently!
- Use plastic containers as much as possible.
- Provide an area to keep materials that will be used during more than one experiment.
- Go over set up, experiment, and clean-up procedures carefully each time you do an experiment.

## Portfolios

Before you begin doing these experiments with your children, create individual portfolios in which they can keep their record sheets for each experiment. Decide where the portfolios will be kept. These provide a place for children to review what they have been doing, and a way for you to check on their progress.

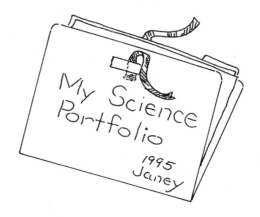

# General Directions for Experiments

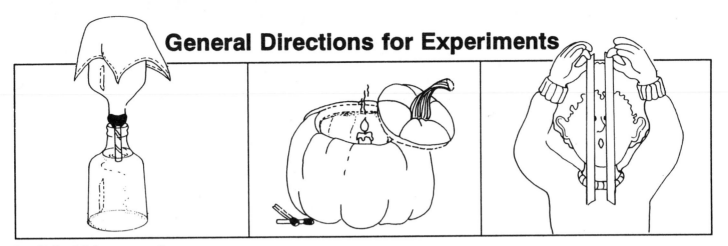

I. Call children together.

    A. Read and discuss the problem.
    B. Show the materials and explain how they will be used.
    C. Pass out the Student Scientific Method sheets and Individual Student Predictor to each child.
    D. Go over the hypotheses choices listed on the Student Scientific Method sheet.

II. Children predict the outcome using their individual predictors and marking their Scientific Method sheet.

    A. The teacher glues the predictors onto the graph as children watch, silently keeping track of how many predictions there are for each choice.
    B. Discuss the graph with your students. Here are some ideas you might use:

        1. Have children tell the scientific reason for making their particular choice.
        2. How many predictions are there for each choice?
        3. Which choice has the most votes?
        4. Which choice has the fewest votes?
        5. How many predictions are there in all?
        6. How many more children predicted A than B?

III. Teacher does the experiment in front of the class. (Or have students get together in small groups to do the experiment.)

    A. Discuss each step.
    B. Describe what is happening.
    C. Explain why it is happening.

IV. Students complete the scientific method worksheet.

    A. The teacher and the class list materials on the chalkboard. Children copy the list.
    B. Write or complete a sentence to answer the conclusion section explaining what actually happened. Children copy this sentence on their forms.
    C. Students draw a picture of the experiment.

V. Display the graph and some of the student's worksheets on a science bulletin board. These can be changed each time you conduct an experiment.

# Good Clean Fun
## Teacher Information Sheet

**Objective:** To teach that soapy water has less surface tension than plain water

**Problem:** What will happen to a paper boat floating on a plate of water when liquid detergent is dropped onto its stern?

Soap will break the surface tension of water. For this reason, paper boats will travel forward when liquid detergent is dropped on the stern. As the surface splits behind the boat, the boat is carried forward on the retreating water "skin." Use the shapes on page 10 as the pattern for your boats.

**Materials Needed:** (*Indicates student worksheet answers)

1. Student Scientific Method sheet
2. Individual Student Predictor
3. Classroom graph
* 4. Paper boat
* 5. Liquid detergent
* 6. Plastic knife or toothpick
* 7. Water
* 8. Plate

## Teaching Procedure:

1. Show students materials to be used in the experiment and state the problem.
2. Pass out individual student predictors and method sheet. Students mark their hypothesis.
3. Chart all student predictions on a class graph. Ask volunteers to explain the reasons for their predictions.
4. Discuss the graph with the class focusing on mathematical concepts.
5. Conduct the experiment. (See "Procedure" on the Scientific Method sheet.)
6. Discuss results as explained in the objective.
7. Have the class complete the student Scientific Method sheet.

## Try this for fun:

Try cutting a slot in one side of the boat. This should make the boat travel in a circle.

**Example of a classroom graph:**

Fold a piece of butcher paper in half and sketch the outline. Cut it out. Plain tag can be used for a simple pictograph.

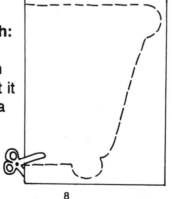

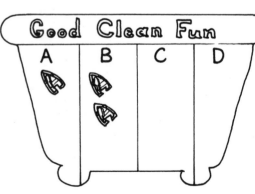

Good Clean Fun

A    B    C    D

8                      How to Do Experiments with Children

Name: _____

## Scientific Method
## Good Clean Fun

**Problem:** What will happen to a paper boat floating on a plate of water when liquid detergent is dropped into its stern?

**Collect Materials:**

1. _____     4. _____

2. _____     5. _____

3. _____

**Hypothesis:** The boat will _____ .

    A. sink
    B. flip over
    C. travel forward
    D. travel backward

**Procedure:** Launch your boat on a plate of water. Place a little detergent on a knife and drop it carefully in the stern. Watch what happens.

**Conclusion:** The boat _____

_____

Draw a picture of our experiment:

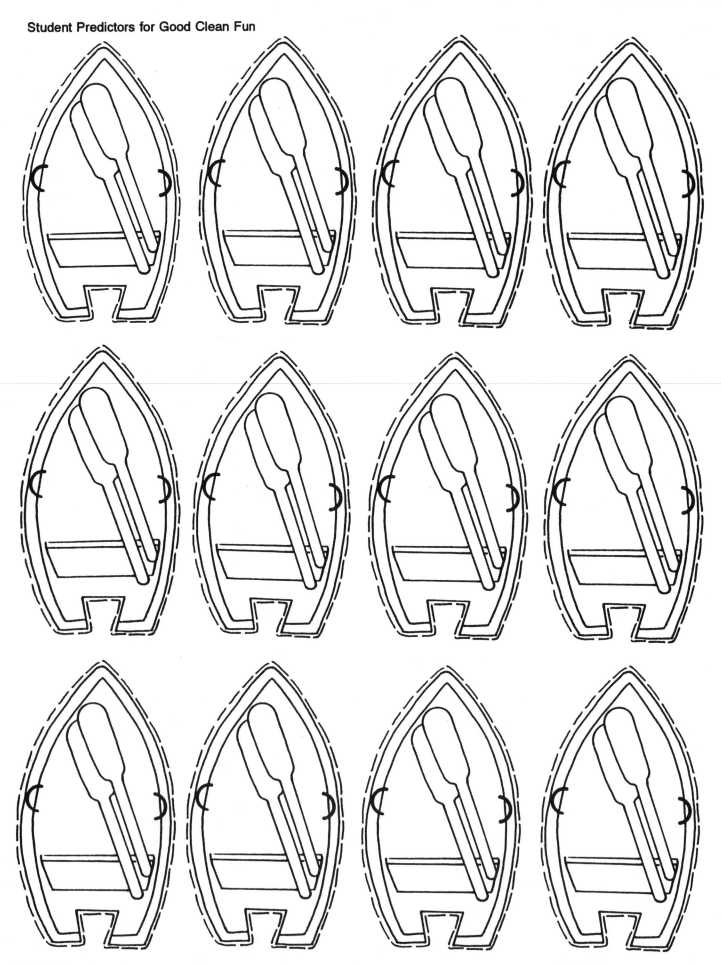

How to Do Experiments with Children

# All Washed Up
## Teacher Information Sheet

**Objective:** To teach that a detergent reduces the surface tension of water

**Problem:** What will happen to a newspaper man when he is put into soapy water, compared to one put in plain water?

Detergent added to water reduces the surface tension. The molecules tend to break apart making the water seem "wetter". In this experiment both paper "men" begin to sink, but the "man" in the soapy water sinks faster because the "wetter" water soaks into the paper fibers more quickly.

**Materials Needed:**  (*Indicates student worksheet answers)

1. Student Scientific Method sheet
2. Individual Student Predictor
3. Classroom graph
* 4. Two glasses
* 5. Dishwashing soap
* 6. Newspaper men
* 7. Water

**Teaching Procedure:**

1. Show students materials to be used in the experiment and state the problem.
2. Pass out individual student predictors and method sheet. Students mark their hypothesis.
3. Chart all student predictions on a class graph. Ask volunteers to explain the reasons for their predictions.
4. Discuss the graph with the class focusing on mathematical concepts.
5. Conduct the experiment. (See "Procedure" on the Scientific Method sheet.)
6. Discuss results as explained in the objective.
7. Have the class complete the student Scientific Method sheet.

**Try this for fun:**

Try different types of soap such as bar soap, powdered detergent, shampoo, and bubble bath.

**Example of a classroom graph:**

Fold a piece of butcher paper in half and sketch the outline. Cut it out. Plain tag can be used for a simple pictograph.

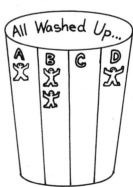

Name: _____

## Scientific Method
## All Washed Up

**Problem:** What will happen to a newspaper man when he is put into soapy water, compared to one put in plain water.

**Collect Materials:**

1. _____    3. _____

2. _____    4. _____

**Hypothesis:** The newspaper man put in soapy water _____ .

        A. floats
        B. sinks faster
        C. sinks slower
        D. sinks at the same speed

**Procedure:** Fill two glasses with tap water. Add soap to one of them. Hold a paper man over each glass. Put them into the water. Watch!

**Conclusion:** The man in soapy water _____

_____

Draw a picture of our experiment:

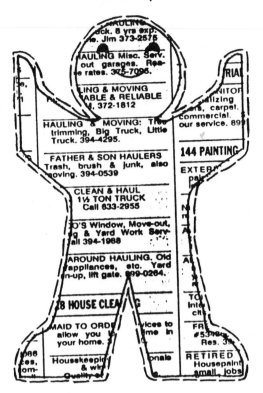

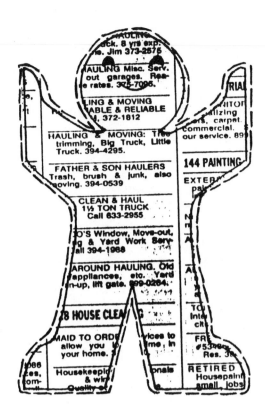

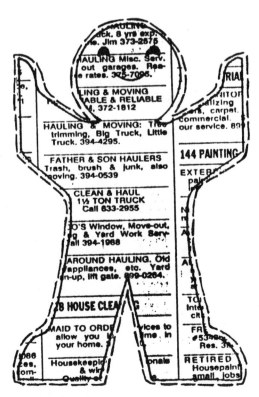

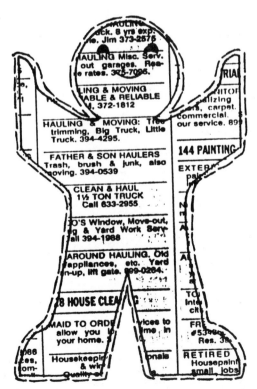

How to Do Experiments with Children

# Take a Powder
## Teacher Information Sheet

**Objective:** To teach that soap breaks down the surface tension of water

**Problem:** What will soap do to baby powder that is floating on water?

Soaps and detergents clean things because they break the surface tension of water. This surface tension is like an invisible skin formed by the strong molecular bond existing between water molecules. When the soap dissolves in the water, it breaks the tension and the powder will be pulled to the sides opposite the soap. This experiment is great to do on an overhead projector.

**Materials Needed:** (* Indicates student worksheet answers)

1. Student Scientific Method sheet
2. Individual Student Predictor
3. Classroom graph
*4. Powder
*5. Plate
*6. Water
*7. Paper clip
*8. Bar of soap

**Teaching Procedure:**

1. Show students materials to be used in the experiment and state the problem.
2. Pass out individual student predictors and method sheet. Students mark their hypothesis.
3. Chart all student predictions on a class graph. Ask volunteers to explain the reasons for their predictions.
4. Discuss the graph with the class focusing on mathematical concepts.
5. Conduct the experiment. (See "Procedure" on the Scientific Method sheet.)
6. Discuss results as explained in the objective.
7. Have the class complete the student Scientific Method sheet.

**Try this for fun:**

Try a drop of liquid detergent and black pepper grains instead of powder.

**Example of a classroom graph:**

Plain tag can be used for a simple pictograph.

Name: _____

## Scientific Method
## Take a Powder

**Problem:** What will soap do to baby powder that is floating on water?

**Collect Materials:**

1. _____    4. _____

2. _____    5. _____

3. _____

**Hypothesis:** The baby powder will _____ .

        A. spread out
        B. dissolve
        C. adhere to the paper clip
        D. blow away

**Procedure:** Sprinkle baby powder over a plate filled with water. Straighten out a paper clip and rub it on the bar of soap. Place it straight into the center of the dish. Watch what happens!

**Conclusion:** The baby powder _____

_____

Draw a picture of our experiment:

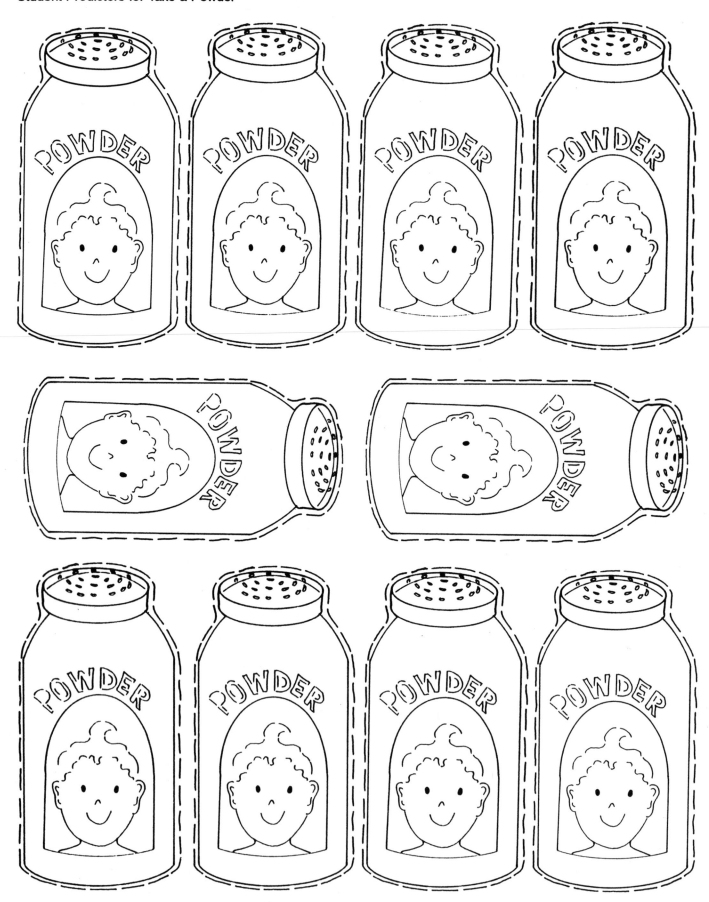

# The Penny Spill
## Teacher Information Sheet

**Objective:** To teach that water has a strong surface bond (surface tension)

**Problem:** How many pennies will it take to make the water spill over the top of the bowl?

Water is made up of many tiny molecules. These molecules have a strong attraction for one another. The molecules at the surface have no water above them so they are attracted downward. This surface tension keeps the water from spilling over the top. The "skin" will stretch, but eventually the number of pennies will make it reach the breaking point and the water will spill over. Use a bowl with sloping sides to allow pennies to slip gently downward.

**Materials Needed:** (* Indicates student worksheet answers)

1. Student Scientific Method Sheet
2. Individual Student Predictor
3. Classroom graph

* 4. A bowl
* 5. Water
* 6. Pennies

**Teaching Procedure:**

1. Show students materials to be used in the experiment and state the problem.
2. Pass out individual student predictors and method sheet. Students mark their hypothesis.
3. Chart all student predictions on a class graph. Ask volunteers to explain the reasons for their predictions.
4. Discuss the graph with the class focusing on mathematical concepts.
5. Conduct the experiment. (See "Procedure" on the Scientific Method sheet.)
6. Discuss results as explained in the objective.
7. Have the class complete the student Scientific Method sheet.

**Try this for fun:**

Use dimes, nickels, or quarters to see if the number of coins will change.
An interesting variation is to drop water onto a penny with an eyedropper to see how many drops it takes before the dome of water breaks.

**Example of a classroom graph:**

Fold a piece of butcher paper in half and sketch the outline of a bowl. Cut it out. Plain tag may be used for a simple pictograph.

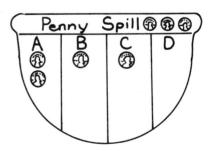

Name: _____

# Scientific Method
# The Penny Spill

**Problem:** How many pennies will it take to make the water spill over the top of the bowl?

**Collect Materials:**

1. _____

2. _____

3. _____

**Hypothesis:** It will take _____ pennies.

> A. under 10
> B. between 11 and 99
> C. more than 100
> D. The water will never overflow.

**Procedure:** Fill a bowl all the way to the top with water. Slowly slide pennies into the water one at a time. Count carefully!

**Conclusion:** It took _____ pennies to make the water overflow.

Draw a picture of our experiment:

 How to Do Experiments with Children

# Surf's Up

**Objective:** To teach that liquids of different densities don't mix.

**Problem:** What happens when water is mixed with oil?

Oil is lighter (less dense) than water and will not mix with it. The water and oil will separate and when gently rocked back and forth will look like a "wave" in the jar. Be sure you have a tight-fitting lid on your jar. Use baby food jars so each child can have the fun of making his/her own wave.

**Materials Needed:** (*Indicates student worksheet answers)

1. Student Scientific Method sheet
2. Individual Student Predictor
3. Classroom graph
* 4. Jar
* 5. Water
* 6. Oil
* 7. Food coloring

## Teaching Procedure:

1. Show students materials to be used in the experiment and state the problem.
2. Pass out individual student predictors and method sheet. Students mark their hypothesis.
3. Chart all student predictions on a class graph. Ask volunteers to explain the reasons for their predictions.
4. Discuss the graph with the class focusing on mathematical concepts.
5. Conduct the experiment. (See "Procedure" on the Scientific Method sheet.)
6. Discuss results as explained in the objective.
7. Have the class complete the student Scientific Method sheet.

## Try this for fun:

Try water dyed with various colors of food coloring for seasonal activities. Make the mix by adding a few drops of liquid detergent and shake vigorously. Try using different types of oil.

## Example of a classroom graph:

Fold a piece of butcher paper in half and sketch the outline shown below. Cut it out. Plain tag can be used for a simple pictograph.

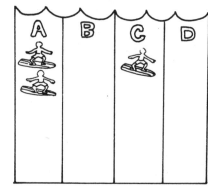

Name: _____

## Scientific Method
## Surf's Up

**Problem:** What happens when water is mixed with oil?

**Collect Materials:**

1. _____    3. _____

2. _____    4. _____

**Hypothesis:** The water and oil will _____ .

        A. mix and change color
        B. become cloudy
        C. separate
        D. form a solid

**Procedure:** Fill a glass jar 3/4 full with water. Add a few drops of food color. Then fill the jar the rest of the way with oil. Place the lid on and gently rock the jar.

**Conclusion:** The water and oil _____

_____

Draw a picture of our experiment:

How to Do Experiments with Children

# Let It Drop
## Teacher Information Sheet

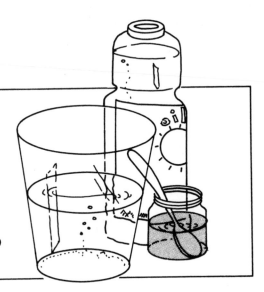

**Objective:** To teach that liquids of different densities don't mix.

**Problem:** What will happen to the drops of colored water when added to the vegetable oil?

Oil is lighter (less dense) than water and will not mix with it. The drops of colored water will eventually sink to the bottom of the oil, retaining their shape as droplets.

**Materials Needed:** (* Indicates student worksheet answers)

1. Student Scientific Method Sheet
2. Individual Student Predictor
3. Classroom graph

  * 4. Food coloring
  * 5. Spoon
  * 6. Water

  * 8. Glass
  * 7. Vegetable oil

**Teaching Procedure:**

1. Show students materials to be used in the experiment and state the problem.
2. Pass out individual student predictors and method sheet. Students mark their hypothesis.
3. Chart all student predictions on a class graph. Ask volunteers to explain the reasons for their predictions.
4. Discuss the graph with the class focusing on mathematical concepts.
5. Conduct the experiment. (See "Procedure" on the Scientific Method sheet.)
6. Discuss results as explained in the objective.
7. Have the class complete the student Scientific Method sheet.

**Try this for fun:**

After doing the experiment, dump all of the colored water into the glass of salad oil. The oil will float to the top of the water.

**Example of a classroom graph:**

Fold a piece of butcher paper in half and sketch the outline. Cut it out. Plain tag may be used for a simple pictograph, if desired.

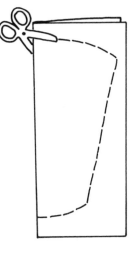

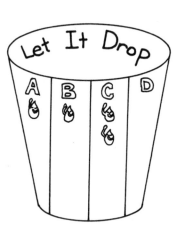

Name: _____

## Scientific Method
## Let it Drop

**Problem:** What will happen to the drops of colored water when added to the vegetable oil?

**Collect Materials:**

1. _____    4. _____

2. _____    5. _____

3. _____

**Hypothesis:** The colored droplets will _____.

        A.  mix with the oil and lose their color
        B.  remain as colored droplets
        C.  change to clear droplets
        D.  move up and down in the oil

**Procedure:** Fill a clear glass with vegetable oil. Carefully spoon several drops of colored water into the oil. Try different sized drops and watch what happens.

**Conclusion:** The colored droplets _____

_____

Draw a picture of our experiment:

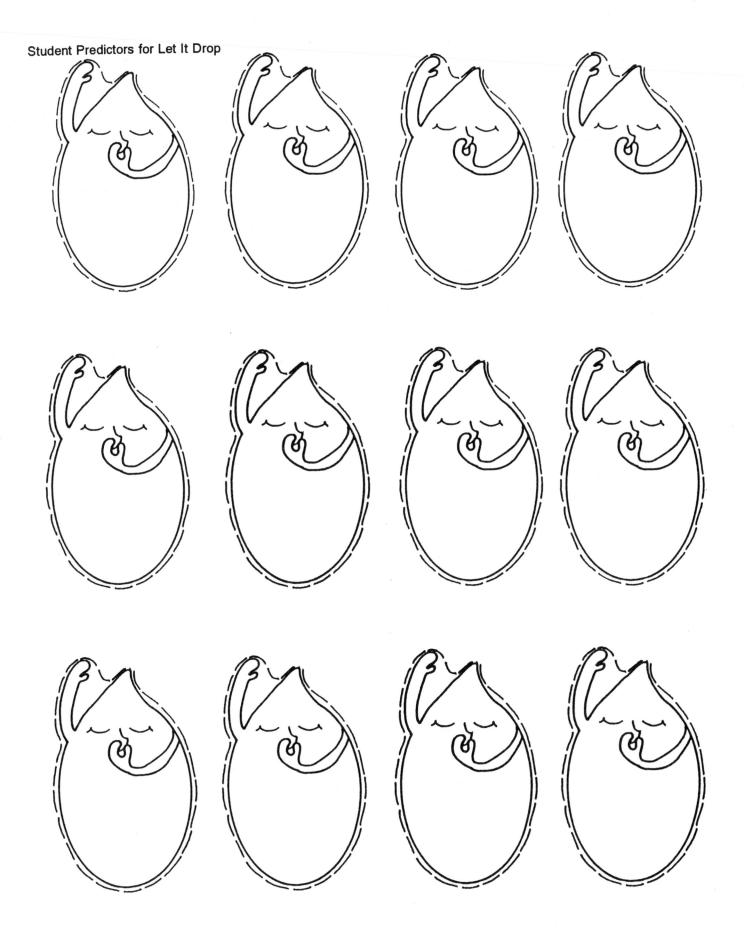

How to Do Experiments with Children

# The Incredible Egg
## Teacher Information Sheet

**Objective:** To teach that liquids have different densities

**Problem:** Which solutions will make the egg float?

Salt water is denser than fresh water. The density of an uncooked egg is slightly greater than fresh water, but less than the density of salt water. Thus, the egg will float in the denser salt water and sink in the other combinations in the experiment.

**Materials Needed:** (* Indicates student worksheet answers)

1. Student Scientific Method sheet
2. Individual Student Predictor
3. Classroom graph

*4. Salt
*5. Water
*6. Corn starch
*7. Vinegar

*8. Spoon
*9. Glasses (4)
*10. Eggs (4)
*11. Food color

**Teaching Procedure:**

1. Show students materials to be used in the experiment and state the problem.
2. Pass out individual student predictors and method sheet. Students mark their hypothesis.
3. Chart all student predictions on a class graph. Ask volunteers to explain the reasons for their predictions.
4. Discuss the graph with the class focusing on mathematical concepts.
5. Conduct the experiment. (See "Procedure" on the Scientific Method sheet.)
6. Discuss results as explained in the objective.
7. Have the class complete the student Scientific Method sheet.

**Try this for fun:**

Try a hard-boiled egg.

**Example of a classroom graph:**

Fold a piece of butcher paper in half, and sketch the outline. Cut it out. Plain tag can be used for a simple pictograph.

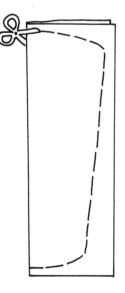

Name: _____

# Scientific Method
# The Incredible Egg

**Problem:** Which solutions will make the egg float?

**Collect Materials:**

1. _____     5. _____

2. _____     6. _____

3. _____     7. _____

4. _____     8. _____

**Hypothesis:** _____ will make the egg float.

  A. Food color and water
  B. Cornstarch and water
  C. Salt and water
  D. Vinegar and water

**Procedure:** Fill each glass 2/3 full of water. Stir in the following ingredients (one per glass). Place a raw egg in each glass.

  • a few drops of food coloring          • two large spoonfuls of salt
  • two large spoonfuls of cornstarch     • two large spoonfuls of vinegar

**Conclusion:** It took a mixture of of _____
to make the egg float.

| Draw a picture of our experiment |
| --- |
|  |

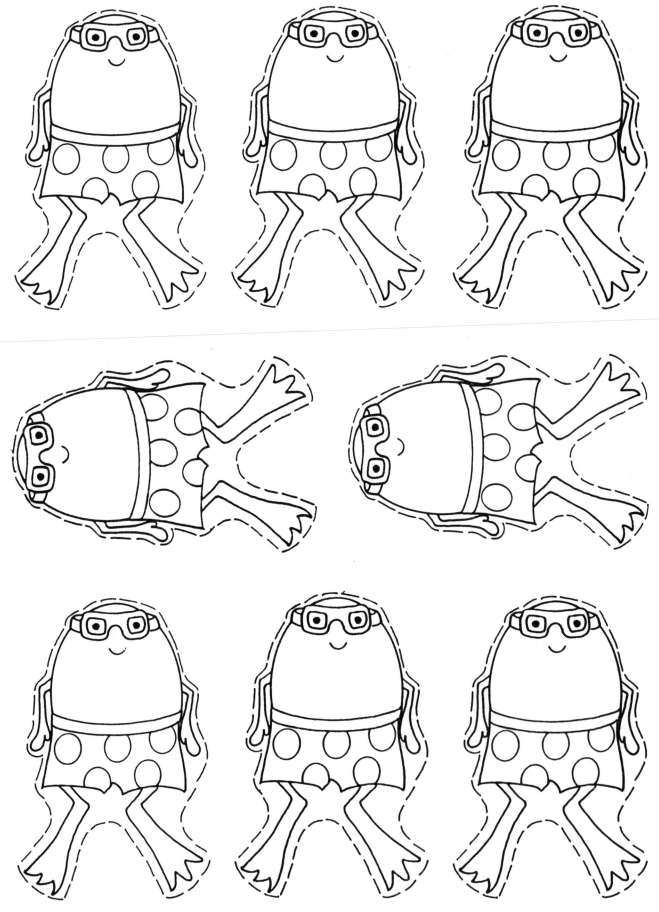

How to Do Experiments with Children

# A Chip Off the Old Potato

## Teacher Information Sheet

**Objective:** To teach that a sugar-water solution has greater density than plain water.

**Problem:** What will happen to the end of a potato floating on a sugar-water solution when you add plain water?

The piece of potato will float or suspend between the sugar water and the fresh water because the potato is more dense than plain water and less dense than the sugar solution. The potato sinks to the bottom of the fresh water and floats on the layer of sugar water. Be sure to pour the plain water slowly when adding it to the sugar water. (You may want to dye the sugar water to make it show up more clearly.)

**Materials Needed:** (* Indicates student worksheet answers)

1. Student Scientific Method sheet
2. Individual Student Predictor
3. Classroom graph

* 4. Potato
* 5. Water
* 6. Glass

* 7. Spoon
* 8. Sugar
* 9. Cup (for pouring)

**Teaching Procedure:**

1. Show students materials to be used in the experiment and state the problem.
2. Pass out individual student predictors and method sheet. Students mark their hypothesis.
3. Chart all student predictions on a class graph. Ask volunteers to explain the reasons for their predictions.
4. Discuss the graph with the class focusing on mathematical concepts.
5. Conduct the experiment. (See "Procedure" on the Scientific Method sheet.)
6. Discuss results as explained in the objective.
7. Have the class complete the student Scientific Method sheet.

**Try this for fun:**

Try salt instead of sugar.

**Example of a classroom graph:**

Fold a piece of butcher paper in half and sketch the outline. Cut it out. Plain tag may be used for a simple pictograph.

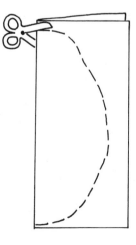
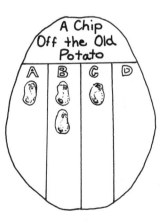

Name: _____

## Scientific Method
## A Chip Off the Old Potato

**Problem:** What will happen to the end of a potato floating on a sugar-water solution when you add plain water?

**Collect materials:**

1. _____   4. _____

2. _____   5. _____

3. _____   6. _____

**Hypothesis:** The end of the potato will _____ .

        A. sink
        B. float on top of the water
        C. suspend in the middle
        D. swell

**Procedure:** Fill a glass 1/2 way with a sugar-water solution. Drop in the potato end. It will float. Now tilt the glass and slowly add plain water to fill the glass.

**Conclusion:** The potato end _____

_____

Draw a picture of our experiment:

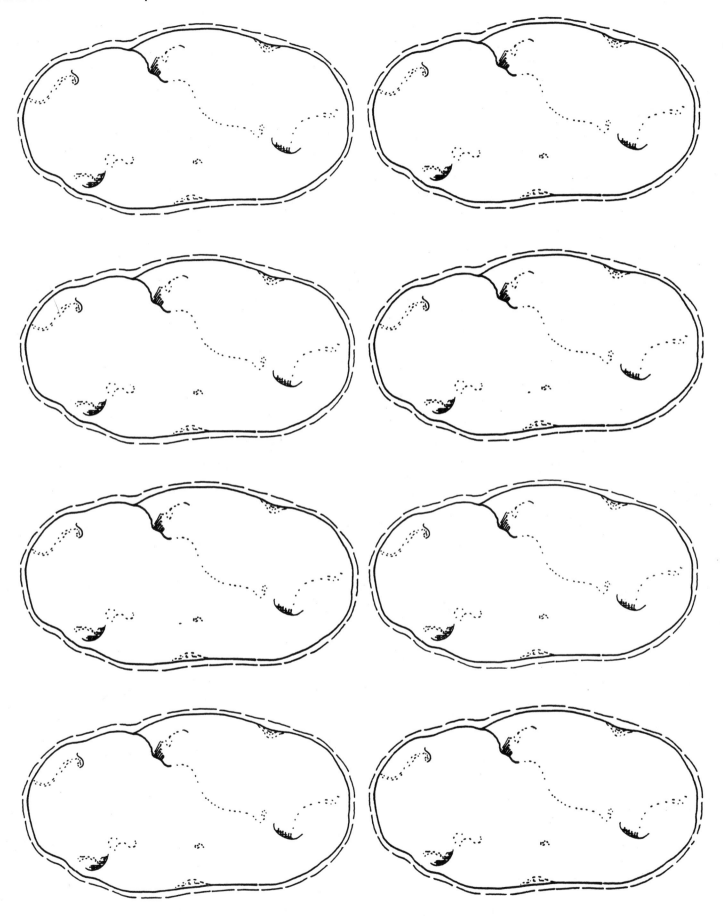

How to Do Experiments with Children

# Dancing Raisins
## Teacher Information Sheet

**Objective:** To teach that a substance less dense than water will float

**Problem:** What will happen to the raisins when you mix them with 7-Up?

Raisins are denser than water so they sink. The 7-Up contains bubbles of carbon dioxide which are less dense than water. The bubbles collect on the raisins causing them to float. When they reach the surface, the bubbles pop and the raisins sink to the bottom again. More bubbles form and they "dance" again. Use regular 7-Up, not the diet type. The experiment works more quickly if one shakes the can first. (Be careful when you open the can.)

**Materials Needed:** (*Indicates student worksheet answers)

1. Student Scientific Method sheet
2. Individual Student Predictor
3. Classroom graph

* 4. 7-Up
* 5. Glass
* 6. Raisins

**Teaching Procedure:**

1. Show students materials to be used in the experiment and state the problem.
2. Pass out individual student predictors and method sheet. Students mark their hypothesis.
3. Chart all student predictions on a class graph. Ask volunteers to explain the reasons for their predictions.
4. Discuss the graph with the class focusing on mathematical concepts.
5. Conduct the experiment. (See "Procedure" on the Scientific Method sheet.)
6. Discuss results as explained in the objective.
7. Have the class complete the student Scientific Method sheet.

**Try this for fun:**

Try various kinds of small fruit and different brands of soda.

**Example of a classroom graph:**

Plain tag may be used for a simple pictograph.

Name: _____

## Scientific Method
## Dancing Raisins

**Problem:** What will happen to the raisins when you mix them with "7-Up"?

**Collect Materials:**

1. _____

2. _____

3. _____

**Hypothesis:** The raisins will _____ .

        A. dissolve
        B. sink and explode
        C. dance up and down
        D. float

**Procedure:** Pour "7-Up" into a clear glass. Drop several raisins in the glass and watch what happens.

**Conclusion:** The raisins will_____

_____

Draw a picture of our experiment.

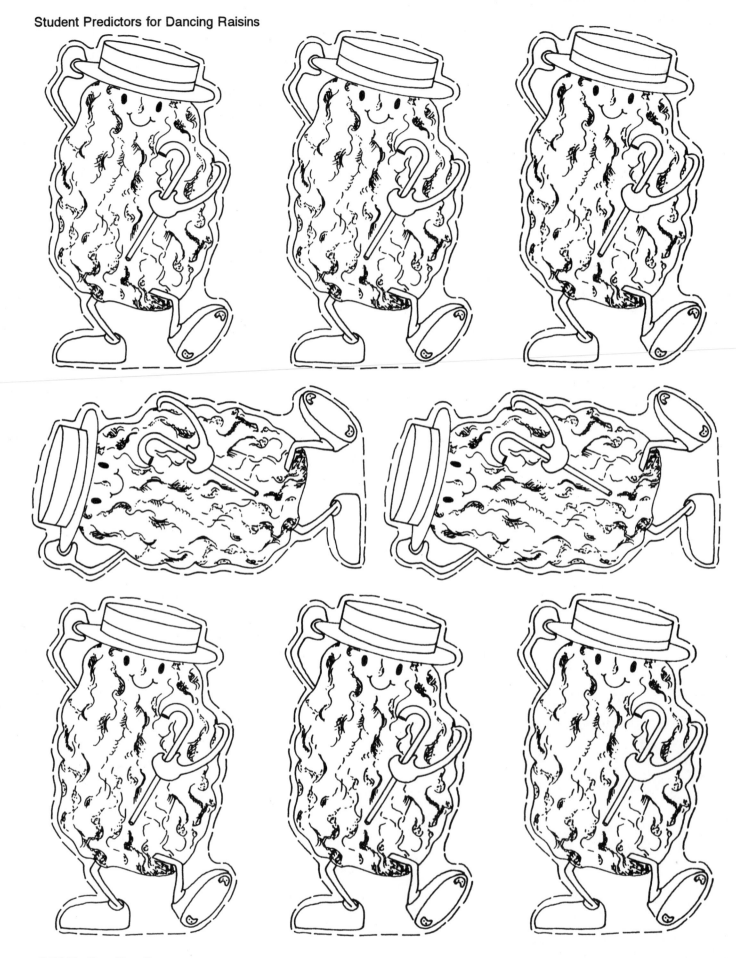

How to Do Experiments with Children

# Great Eggs-pectations
## Teacher Information Sheet

**Objective:** To teach that objects float more readily in salt water than fresh water as salt water has greater density

**Problem:** What will happen to an egg in a glass full of water when salt is added to it?

Salt water is more dense than fresh water. The density of an egg is slightly greater than fresh water, so the egg sinks. The egg is slightly less dense than salt water, so the egg will float in salt water.

**Materials Needed:** (*Indicates student worksheet answers)

1. Student Scientific Method sheet    * 4. Egg    * 7. Salt
2. Individual Student Predictor    * 5. Glass    * 8. Spoon
3. Classroom graph    * 6. Water

**Teaching Procedure:**

1. Show students materials to be used in the experiment and state the problem.
2. Pass out individual student predictors and method sheet. Students mark their hypothesis.
3. Chart all student predictions on a class graph. Ask volunteers to explain the reasons for their predictions.
4. Discuss the graph with the class focusing on mathematical concepts.
5. Conduct the experiment. (See "Procedure" on the Scientific Method sheet.)
6. Discuss results as explained in the objective.
7. Have the class complete the student Scientific Method sheet.

**Try this for fun:**

Try different objects to see which float or sink. Several types of fruit would work.

**Example of classroom graph:**

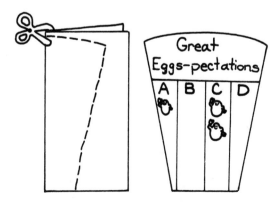

Fold a piece of butcher paper in half and sketch the outline. Cut it out. Plain tag may be used for a simple pictograph.

        How to Do Experiments with Children

Name: _____

# Scientific Method
# Great Eggs-pectations

**Problem:** What will happen to the egg in a glass full of water when salt is added to it?

**Collect Materials:**

1. _____     4. _____

2. _____     5. _____

3. _____

**Hypothesis:** The egg will _____ .

         A. crack open
         B. float
         C. pop out of the glass
         D. change color

**Procedure:** Place an egg in a glass. Fill it with fresh water. Observe the egg. Now add salt to the water. Watch what happens!

**Conclusion:** The egg _____

_____

Draw a picture of our experiment.

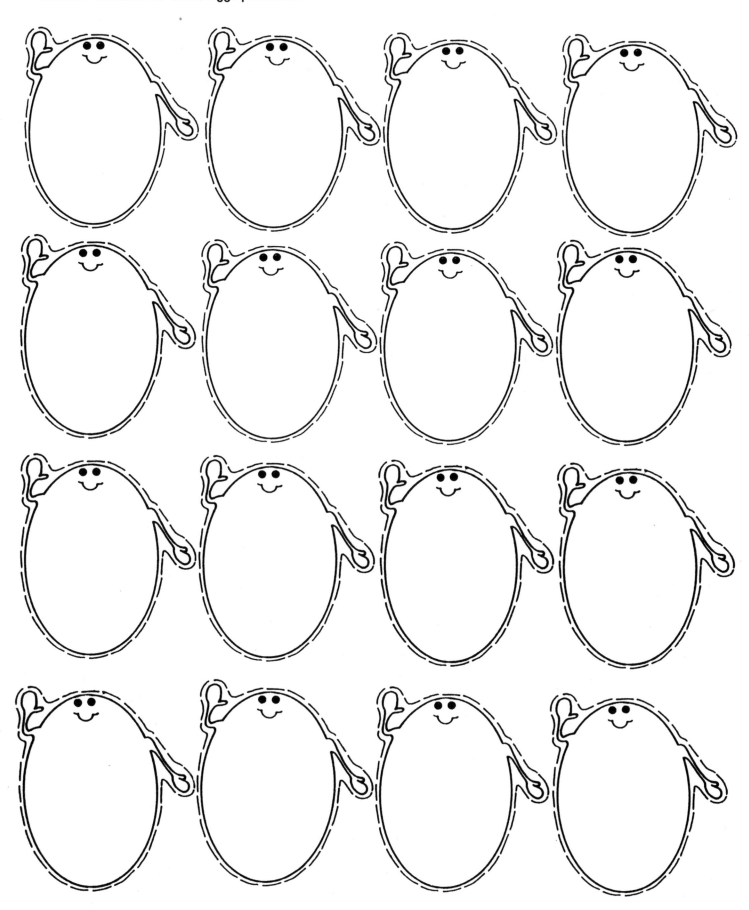

How to Do Experiments with Children

# A Moo-ving Experiment
## Teacher Information Sheet

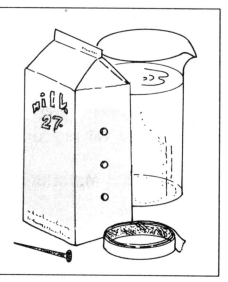

**Objective:** To teach that water pressure increases with depth.

**Problem:** Which of three holes punched one above the other in a milk carton will produce the longest stream of water?

Punch 3 holes in a cardboard milk carton and cover them with tape. Fill it with water and then remove the tape. This experiment will show that the deeper the water, the greater its pressure, and the greater the force with which it pushes. The water coming from the lowest hole will reach out the farthest.

**Materials Needed:** (*Indicates student worksheet answers)

1. Student Scientific Method sheet
2. Individual Student Predictor
3. Classroom graph

* 4. Milk carton
* 5. Tape
* 6. Water
* 7. Nail

**Teaching Procedure:**

1. Show students materials to be used in the experiment and state the problem.
2. Pass out individual student predictors and method sheet. Students mark their hypothesis.
3. Chart all student predictions on a class graph. Ask volunteers to explain the reasons for their predictions.
4. Discuss the graph with the class focusing on mathematical concepts.
5. Conduct the experiment. (See "Procedure" on the Scientific Method sheet.)
6. Discuss results as explained in the objective.
7. Have the class complete the student Scientific Method sheet.

**Try this for fun:**

Try different sized containers and holes.

**Example of a classroom graph:**

Fold a piece of butcher paper in half and sketch the outline. Cut it out. Plain tag can be used for a simple pictograph.

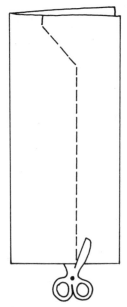

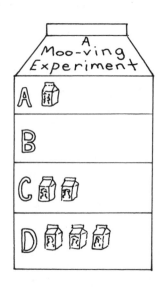

Name: _____

## Scientific Method
## A Moo-ving Experiment

**Problem:** Which of three holes punched one above the other in a milk carton will produce the longest stream of water?

**Collect Materials:**

1. _____    3. _____

2. _____    4. _____

**Hypothesis:** The _____ hole will produce the longest stream of water.

        A. bottom
        B. middle
        C. top
        D. NONE--all will be the same.

**Procedure:** Punch three small holes, one above the other, along the side of an empty milk carton. Cover the holes with tape and fill the carton with water. Pull off the tape and watch what happens.

**Conclusion:** The longest stream was from the _____ hole.

Draw a picture of our experiment:

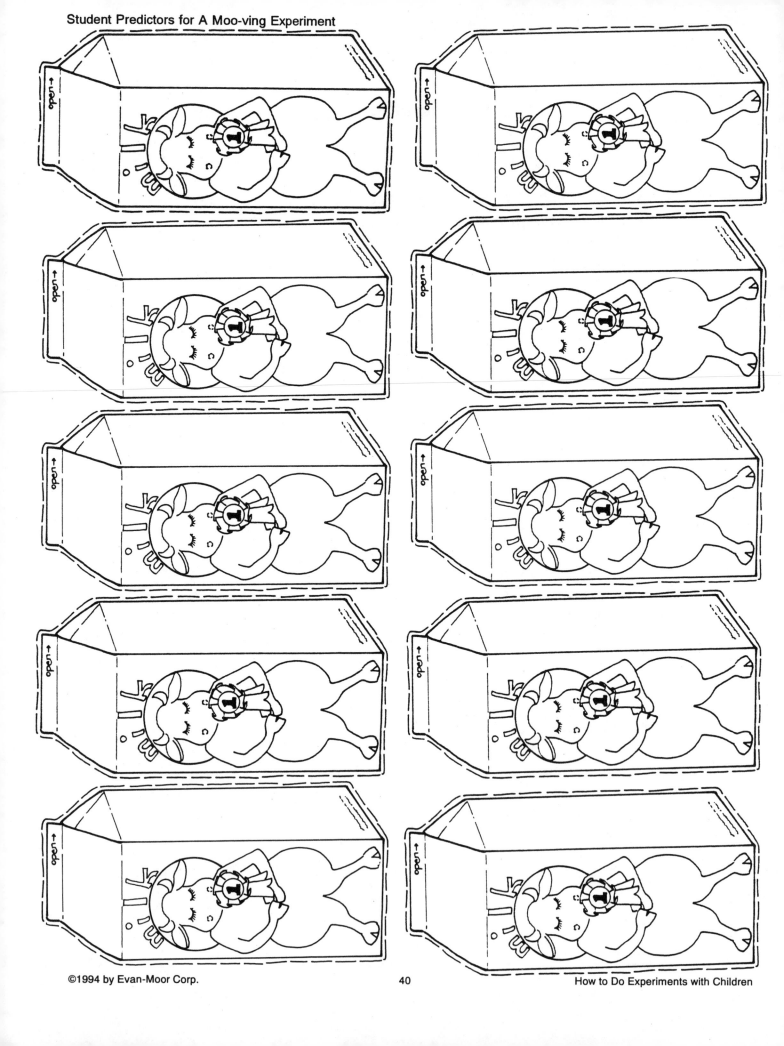

40

How to Do Experiments with Children

# Plip, Plop, Drip, Drop
## Teacher Information Sheet

**Objective:** To teach that cold water sinks and warm water rises

**Problem:** What will happen to cold water when it is emptied into a bowl of warm water?

The cold water will sink to the bottom because it is "heavier" (more dense) than the warm water. The molecules in cold water are tightly compacted so it appears to be heavier. Warm water molecules expand and therefore seem "lighter."

**Materials Needed:** (* Indicates student worksheet answers)

| | | |
|---|---|---|
| 1. Student Scientific Method Sheet | * 4. Bowl | * 7. Food coloring |
| 2. Individual Student Predictor | * 5. Warm water | * 8. Cold water |
| 3. Classroom graph | * 6. Small bottle | * 9. Your thumb |

**Teaching Procedure:**

1. Show students materials to be used in the experiment and state the problem.
2. Pass out individual student predictors and method sheet. Students mark their hypothesis.
3. Chart all student predictions on a class graph. Ask volunteers to explain the reasons for their predictions.
4. Discuss the graph with the class focusing on mathematical concepts.
5. Conduct the experiment. (See "Procedure" on the Scientific Method sheet.)
6. Discuss results as explained in the objective.
7. Have the class complete the student Scientific Method sheet.

**Try this for fun:**

Try it the other way around. Fill a bowl with cold water and pour warm water into it. The warm water will float to the top.

**Example of a classroom graph:**

Fold a piece of butcher paper in half and sketch the outline. Cut it out. Plain tag may be used for a simple pictograph.

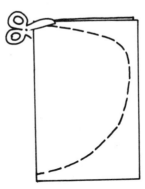

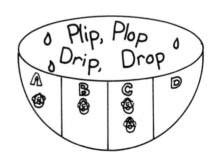

41                    How to Do Experiments with Children

Name: _____

## Scientific Method
## Plip, Plop, Drip, Drop

**Problem:** What will happen to cold water when it is emptied into a bowl of warm water?

**Collect Materials:**

1. _____    4. _____

2. _____    5. _____

3. _____    6. _____

**Hypothesis:** The cold water will _____ .

        A. float on top
        B. mix into the warm water
        C. sink to the bottom
        D. form an ice cube

**Procedure:** Fill a glass bowl with warm water. Fill a small bottle with cold water and add a little food coloring. Hold the bottle sideways and lower it into the warm water. Take away your thumb and watch what happens!

**Conclusion:** The cold water _____

_____

Draw a picture of our experiment:

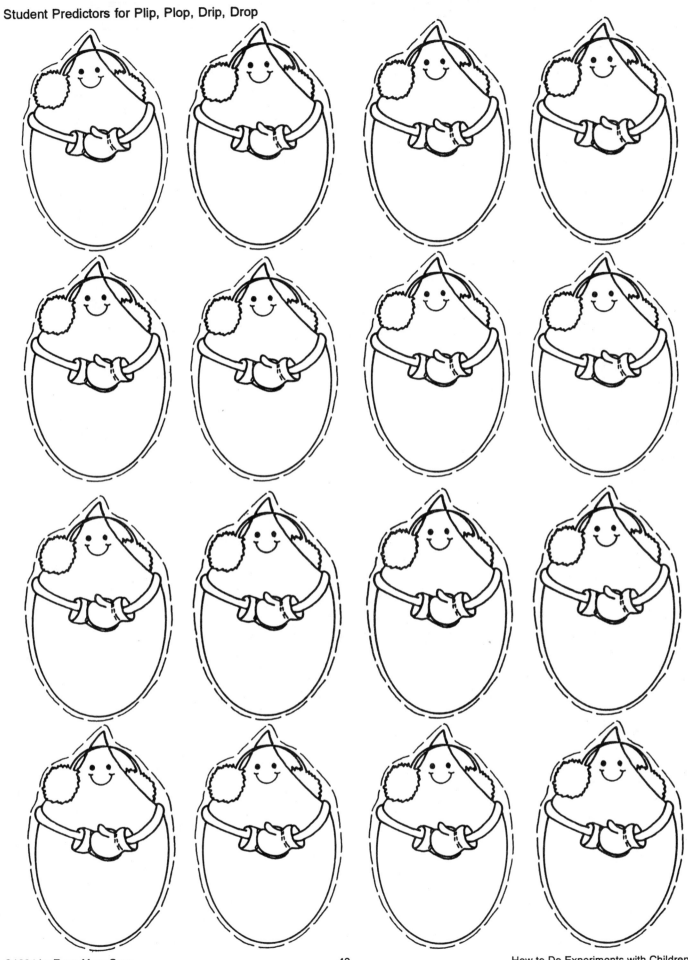

How to Do Experiments with Children

# Water Wonder

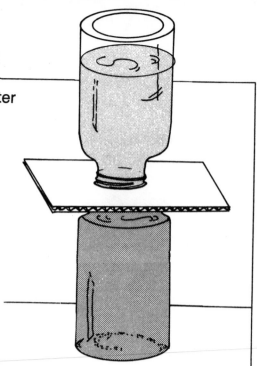

**Objective:** To teach that warm water rises and cold water sinks

**Problem:** What will happen to the colored water in a warm bottle when it is placed on top of a bottle of cold water?

The molecules in warm water are moving apart, causing it to be lighter than cold water. The lighter warm water rises and the heavier cold water sinks. If the warm water is in the top bottle, nothing will happen. The colored water will not mix with the lighter warm water. It will stay on top of the heavier cold water. Use railroad board or lightweight cardboard to put between the two bottles of water. Large baby food jars work well.

**Materials Needed:** (*Indicates student worksheet answers)

1. Student Scientific Method sheet
2. Individual Student Predictor
3. Classroom graph

* 4. Warm water
* 5. Cool water
* 6. Food colors (red & blue)

* 7. Cardboard
* 8. Two bottles

**Teaching Procedure:**

1. Show students materials to be used in the experiment and state the problem.
2. Pass out individual student predictors and method sheet. Students mark their hypothesis.
3. Chart all student predictions on a class graph. Ask volunteers to explain the reasons for their predictions.
4. Discuss the graph with the class focusing on mathematical concepts.
5. Conduct the experiment. (See "Procedure" on the Scientific Method sheet.)
6. Discuss results as explained in the objective.
7. Have the class complete the student Scientific Method sheet.

**Try this for fun:**

Reverse the bottles, putting the cold bottle on top. The warm water will mix with the cold and change the color to purple.

**Example of a classroom graph:**

Fold a piece of butcher paper in half and sketch the outline. Cut it out. Plain tag can be used for a simple pictograph.

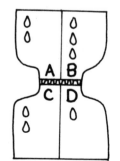

44          How to Do Experiments with Children

Name: _____

# Scientific Method
# Water Wonder

**Problem:** What will happen to the colored water in a warm bottle when it is placed on top of a bottle of cold water?

**Collect Materials:**

1. _____    4. _____

2. _____    5. _____

3. _____

**Hypothesis:** The water in the warm bottle will _____ .

        A. mix with the cold and turn purple
        B. evaporate
        C. do nothing
        D. mix with the cold and then steam

**Procedure:** Put a little blue food color in one bottle and fill with cool water. Put a little red food color in the other bottle and fill with warm water. Hold the cardboard over the top of the red bottle and turn it over on top of the blue one. Carefully pull out the cardboard to see what happens.

**Conclusion:** The warm water will _____

Draw a picture of our experiment:

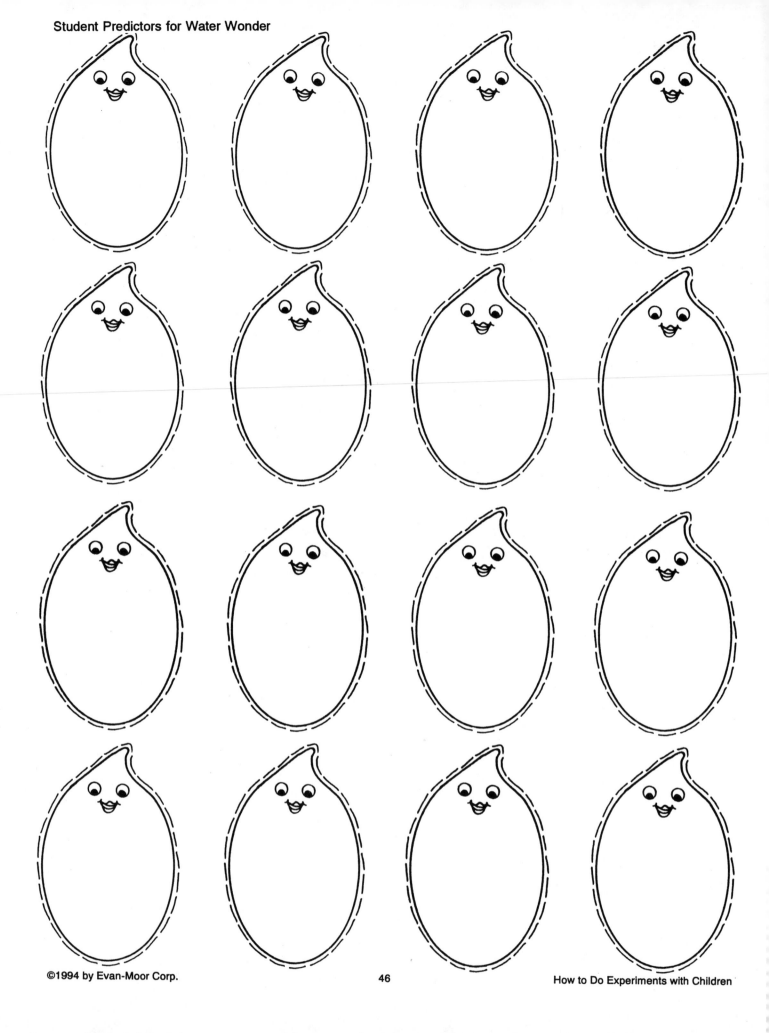

How to Do Experiments with Children

# Mix It Up
## Teacher Information Sheet

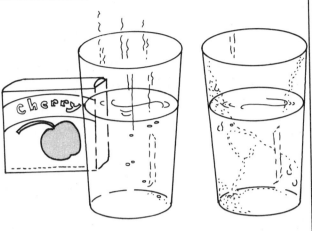

**Objective:** To teach that some substances mix more quickly in hot liquids than in cold liquids

**Problem:** In cold water, a pinch of powdered flavored gelatin will sink and slowly begin to mix with the water. What will happen when a pinch of flavored gelatin is added to hot water?

The molecules in hot water move more quickly than those in cold water. Thus, when the flavored gelatin is added to warm water it swirls and mixes very quickly.

**Materials Needed:** (* Indicates student worksheet answers)

1. Student Scientific Method sheet
2. Individual Student Predictor
3. Classroom graph
*4. Glass

*5. Hot water
*6. Flavored gelatin
*7. Cold water

## Teaching Procedure:

1. Show students materials to be used in the experiment and state the problem.
2. Pass out individual student predictors and method sheet. Students mark their hypothesis.
3. Chart all student predictions on a class graph. Ask volunteers to explain the reasons for their predictions.
4. Discuss the graph with the class focusing on mathematical concepts.
5. Conduct the experiment. (See "Procedure" on the Scientific Method sheet.)
6. Discuss results as explained in the objective.
7. Have the class complete the student Scientific Method sheet.

## Try this for fun:

Try a powdered drink mix.

## Example of a classroom graph:

Plain tag can be used for a simple pictograph.

Name: _____

## Scientific Method
## Mix It Up

**Problem:** In cold water, a pinch of powdered flavored gelatin will sink and slowly begin to mix with the water. What will happen when a pinch of flavored gelatin is added to hot water?

**Collect Materials:**

1. _____    3. _____

2. _____    4. _____

**Hypothesis:** In hot water the powdered flavored gelatin _____

_____.

      A. will swirl and quickly mix with the water
      B. will make delicious gelatin
      C. will instantly harden
      D. will react the same as in the cold water

**Procedure:** Fill a glass with cold water and watch the gelatin's reaction. Now fill another glass with hot tap water and add a pinch of flavored gelatin.

**Conclusion:** The powdered gelatin in hot water _____

_____

Draw a picture of our experiment:

How to Do Experiments with Children

**Note:** This is fun to do at the beginning of the school year.

# What Do I See?
## Teacher Information Sheet

**Objective:** To teach that light rays "bend" when passing from one substance to another (refraction).

**Problem:** How will a pencil look when it is placed in a glass 1/2 full of water?

The pencil appears to be broken because the light returning from the parts of the pencil below the water bends when it hits the water surface. The side of the pencil not in the water is seen from a different direction. Thus, the pencil appears to be broken. Be sure to stand so you can see the side and top of the water.

**Materials Needed:** (* Indicates student worksheet answers)

1. Student Scientific Method sheet
2. Individual Student Predictor
3. Classroom graph

* 4. Glass
* 5. Pencil
* 6. Water

**Teaching Procedure:**

1. Show students materials to be used in the experiment and state the problem.
2. Pass out individual student predictors and method sheet. Students mark their hypothesis.
3. Chart all student predictions on a class graph. Ask volunteers to explain the reasons for their predictions.
4. Discuss the graph with the class focusing on mathematical concepts.
5. Conduct the experiment. (See "Procedure" on the Scientific Method sheet.)
6. Discuss results as explained in the objective.
7. Have the class complete the student Scientific Method sheet.

**Try this for fun:**

Try different objects.

**Example of a classroom graph:**

Fold a piece of butcher paper in half and sketch the outline. Cut it out. Plain tag may be used for a simple pictograph, if desired.

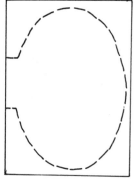
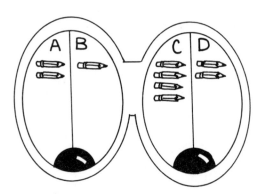

Name: _____

## Scientific Method
## What Do I See?

**Problem:** How will a pencil look when it is placed in a glass 1/2 full of water?

**Collect Materials:**

1. _____

2. _____

3. _____

**Hypothesis:** The pencil _____ .

        A. appears to move up and down
        B. appears to be writing a message
        C. appears to be broken
        D. changes color

**Procedure:** Fill a glass 1/2 full of water. Place a pencil in the glass. Stand so that you can see the top and side of the water. Look carefully!

**Conclusion:** The pencil _____

_____

Draw a picture of our experiment:

52

How to Do Experiments with Children

# No Vacancy

## Teacher Information Sheet

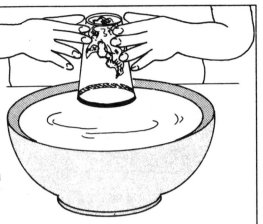

**Objective:** To teach that air occupies space

**Problem:** What will happen to a napkin in a glass when the glass is placed in a bowl of water?

This experiment shows that air occupies space. A crumpled paper napkin pushed into a glass will remain dry when the glass is pushed straight down into a bowl of water. The air is trapped inside and there is no room for the water to get in. This shows the glass was full of something even though you could not see it.

**Materials Needed:** (*Indicates student worksheet answers)

1. Student Scientific Method sheet
2. Individual Student Predictor
3. Classroom graph

* 4. Napkin
* 5. Glass
* 6. Bowl
* 7. Water

## Teaching Procedure:

1. Show students materials to be used in the experiment and state the problem.
2. Pass out individual student predictors and method sheet. Students mark their hypothesis.
3. Chart all student predictions on a class graph. Ask volunteers to explain the reasons for their predictions.
4. Discuss the graph with the class focusing on mathematical concepts.
5. Conduct the experiment. (See "Procedure" on the Scientific Method sheet.)
6. Discuss results as explained in the objective.
7. Have the class complete the student Scientific Method sheet.

## Try this for fun:

Try tipping the glass while it is under the water. Watch out! (This proves that air was trapped in the glass from the beginning.)

## Example of a classroom graph:

Fold a piece of butcher paper in half and sketch the outline. Cut it out. Plain tag can be used for a simple pictograph.

Name: _____

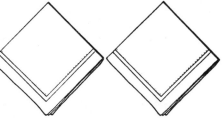

## Scientific Method
## No Vacancy

**Problem:** What will happen to a napkin in a glass when the glass is placed in a bowl of water?

**Collect Material:**

1. _____     3. _____

2. _____     4. _____

**Hypothesis:** The napkin will_____ .

        A. stay dry
        B. get soggy
        C. disintegrate
        D. absorb all the water in the bowl

**Procedure:** Crumple a napkin and push it in the bottom of a glass. Turn the glass upside down into the bowl of water. Pull the glass out. What happened to the napkin?

**Conclusion:** The napkin _____

_____

Draw a picture of our experiment:

55

How to Do Experiments with Children

# Blow Out
## Teacher Information Sheet

**Objective:** To teach that air occupies space

**Problem:** What will happen to a balloon in a bottle when you blow into it?

Air takes up space and the bottle is full of air!
When you try to blow up the balloon, the air trapped inside the bottle prevents the balloon from inflating.
A soft drink bottle works well.

**Materials Needed:** (* Indicates student worksheet answers)

1. Student Scientific Method Sheet
2. Individual Student Predictor
3. Classroom graph

* 4. Bottle
* 5. Balloon

## Teaching Procedure:

1. Show students materials to be used in the experiment and state the problem.
2. Pass out individual student predictors and method sheet. Students mark their hypothesis.
3. Chart all student predictions on a class graph. Ask volunteers to explain the reasons for their predictions.
4. Discuss the graph with the class focusing on mathematical concepts.
5. Conduct the experiment. (See "Procedure" on the Scientific Method sheet.)
6. Discuss results as explained in the objective.
7. Have the class complete the student Scientific Method sheet.

**Try this for fun:**

Try varying the size of the balloons.

**Example of a classroom graph:**

Fold a piece of butcher paper in half and sketch the outline. Cut it out. Plain tag may be used for a simple pictograph.

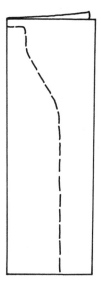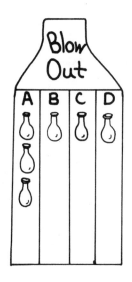

How to Do Experiments with Children

Name: _____

## Scientific Method
## Blow Out

**Problem:** What will happen to a balloon in a bottle when you blow into it?

**Collect Material:**

1. _____

2. _____

**Hypothesis:** The balloon in the bottle will _____.

        A. break the bottle
        B. pop
        C. do nothing
        D. change color

**Procedure:** Push the deflated balloon into the bottle and stretch the open end of the balloon back over the bottle's mouth. Blow as hard as you can!

**Conclusion:** The balloon in the bottle _____

_____

Draw a picture of our experiment:

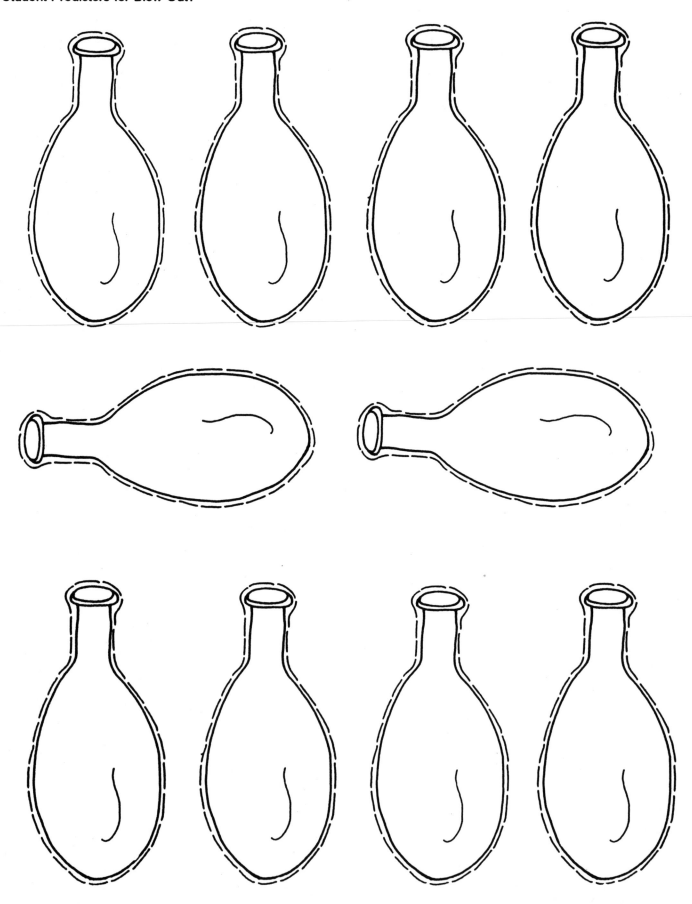

How to Do Experiments with Children

# Under Pressure
## Teacher Information Sheet

**Objective:** To teach that air occupies less space when compressed

**Problem:** What will happen to the eyedropper in the bottle when you push in and pull out the cork?

When you push down on the cork, the air in the eye dropper is compress allowing more water into the eyedropper. Because it is now heavier, it will sink. When the cork is pulled out, the air in the eye dropper expands pushing water out of the eyedropper so it will rise. This is how a submarine works. Be sure to use a <u>glass</u> eyedropper in this experiment.

**Materials Needed:** (* Indicates student worksheet answers)

1. Student Scientific Method sheet
2. Individual Student Predictor
3. Classroom graph

*4. Water
*5. Bottle
*6. Cork

*7. Eyedropper

## Teaching Procedure:

1. Show students materials to be used in the experiment and state the problem.
2. Pass out individual student predictors and method sheet. Students mark their hypothesis.
3. Chart all student predictions on a class graph. Ask volunteers to explain the reasons for their predictions.
4. Discuss the graph with the class focusing on mathematical concepts.
5. Conduct the experiment. (See "Procedure" on the Scientific Method sheet.)
6. Discuss results as explained in the objective.
7. Have the class complete the student Scientific Method sheet.

## Try this for fun:

Try different colors of water for seasonal activities. Try a plastic eyedropper or different sized bottles and corks.

## Example of a classroom graph:

Fold a piece of butcher paper in half, and sketch the outline. Cut it out. Plain tag can be used for a simple pictograph.

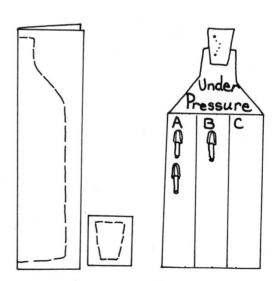

Name: _____

## Scientific Method
## Under Pressure

**Problem:** What will happen to the eyedropper in the bottle when you push in and pull out the cork?

**Collect Materials:**

1. _____    3. _____

2. _____    4. _____

**Hypothesis:** The eyedropper will _____ when the cork is pulled in and out.

A. move up and down
B. do nothing
C. burst

**Procedure:** Fill an eyedropper partially full of water so that it will float. Fill a bottle completely full of water. Place the dropper into the bottle and push the cork in. Watch what happens! Now, pull the cork out. What happens?

**Conclusion:** The eyedropper _____

_____

Draw a picture of our experiment:

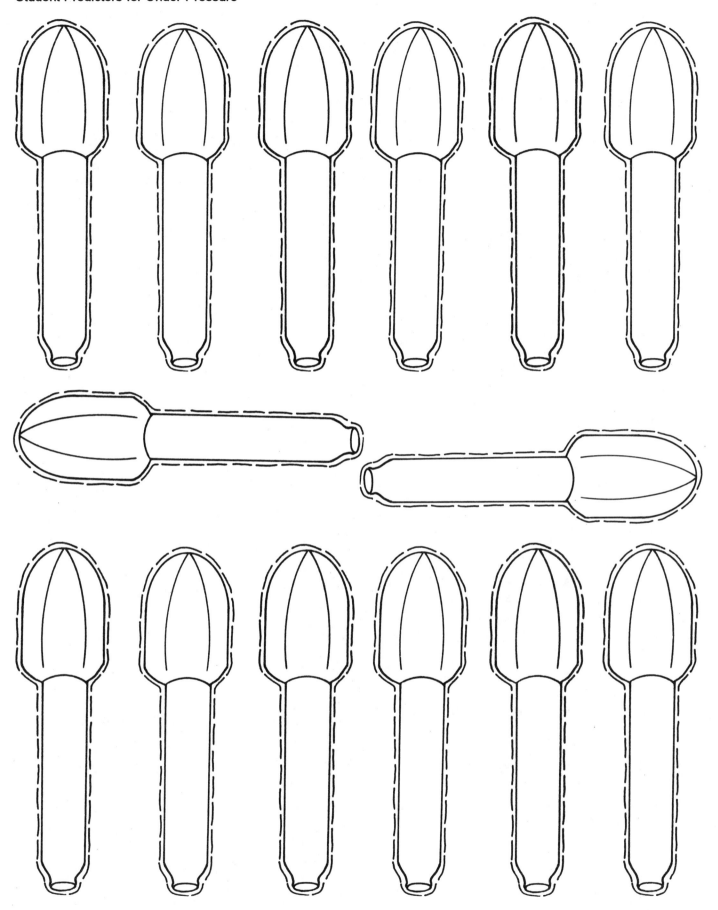

# Rock-a-Bye Bottle
## Teacher Information Sheet

**Objective:** To teach that a gas occupies more space than a liquid

**Problem:** What will happen to a sealed nipple on a baby bottle when it is filled with soda pop and gently rocked back and forth?

When the can of soda is opened, the carbon dioxide gas it contains begins to be released, inflating the nipple. Gently rocking the bottle speeds up the process. You can buy a nipple without a hole in it or apply super glue to the nipple to block the openings. The nipple will eventually inflate enough to hold 8-9 oz. (237-266 ml) of soda. Pour the carbonated drink into a baby bottle and seal it as quickly as you can so you will not lose much of the carbonation.

**Materials Needed:** (* Indicates student worksheet answers)

1. Student Scientific Method sheet
2. Individual Student Predictor
3. Classroom graph

*4. Baby bottle
*5. Holeless nipple
*6. Soda

**Teaching Procedure:**

1. Show students materials to be used in the experiment and state the problem.
2. Pass out individual student predictors and method sheet. Students mark their hypothesis.
3. Chart all student predictions on a class graph. Ask volunteers to explain the reasons for their predictions.
4. Discuss the graph with the class focusing on mathematical concepts.
5. Conduct the experiment. (See "Procedure" on the Scientific Method sheet.)
6. Discuss results as explained in the objective.
7. Have the class complete the student Scientific Method sheet.

**Try this for fun:**

Try with homemade soda water combining varying amounts of baking soda, water and vinegar.

**Example of a classroom graph:**

Plain tag can be used for a simple pictograph.

Rock-A-Bye Bottle

| | |
|---|---|
| A | 🍼 |
| B | 🍼 🍼 |
| C | |
| D | |

Name: _____

## Scientific Method
## Rock-a-Bye Bottle

**Problem:** What will happen to a sealed nipple on a baby bottle when it is filled with soda pop and gently rocked back and forth?

**Collect Materials:**

1. _____     3. _____

2. _____

**Hypothesis:** The sealed nipple _____ .

      A.  will shoot off the top of the bottle
      B.  will be sucked into the bottle
      C.  will expand
      D.  will start to dissolve

**Procedure:** Seal the nipple and fill a bottle with soda. Be sure to screw the top on tight. Gently rock the bottle back and forth. Watch out!

**Conclusion:** The sealed nipple _____

_____

Draw a picture of our experiment:

How to Do Experiments with Children

# Funny Money
## Teacher Information Sheet

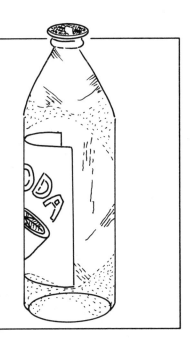

**Objective:** To teach that cold air contracts and warm air expands

**Problem:** What will happen to a nickel when it is placed on top of a soda bottle which has been in the freezer for at least 15 minutes?

Cold air contracts and takes up less space than warm air. This allows the bottle to hold more air than it did at room temperature. Take the bottle out of the freezer and quickly place a wet nickel over the top. Drip a little water around the edge of the bottle to form a seal. As the bottle warms, the cold air inside warms and expands. This expanding gas pressure causes the nickel to lift up and fall back down as the air escapes.

**Materials Needed:** (* Indicates student worksheet answers)

1. Student Scientific Method sheet
2. Individual Student Predictor
3. Classroom graph
*4. Soda bottle
*5. Nickel
*6. Water

**Teaching Procedure:**

1. Show students materials to be used in the experiment and state the problem.
2. Pass out individual student predictors and method sheet. Students mark their hypothesis.
3. Chart all student predictions on a class graph. Ask volunteers to explain the reasons for their predictions.
4. Discuss the graph with the class focusing on mathematical concepts.
5. Conduct the experiment. (See "Procedure" on the Scientific Method sheet.)
6. Discuss results as explained in the objective.
7. Have the class complete the student Scientific Method sheet.

**Try this for fun:**

Hold your hands around the bottle. This will speed up the heating process. Try different sized bottles and coins.

**Example of a classroom graph:**

Plain tag can be used for a simple pictograph.

| Ha Ha Funny Money Ha Ha | | |
|---|---|---|
| A ◉ | | |
| B ◉ | ◉ | |
| C | | |
| D ◉ | | |

Name: _____

# Scientific Method
# Funny Money

**Problem:** What will happen to a nickel when it is placed on top of a soda bottle which has been in the freezer for at least 15 minutes?

**Collect Materials:**

1. _____     3. _____

2. _____

**Hypothesis:** The nickel will _____.

        A. flip over on top of the bottle
        B. fly off the top
        C. be sucked into the bottle
        D. make a popping sound

**Procedure:** Place an empty soda bottle in the freezer for at least 15 minutes. Immediately cover the mouth with a wet nickel. Wet your fingers and let the water drip around the edge of the nickel. Wait!

**Conclusion:** The nickel _____

_____

Draw a picture of our experiment:

How to Do Experiments with Children

How to Do Experiments with Children

**Note:** Try this experiment around Easter.

# Egg Rescue
## Teacher Information Sheet

**Objective:** To teach that the more air that is present, the greater the air pressure

**Problem:** How can we get the hard-boiled egg out of the bottle without breaking the egg or the bottle?

Begin this experiment with a hard-boiled egg in the bottle. (See the experiment on page 98.) Wash out all the charred paper. Hold the bottle upside down being sure the egg is covering the opening. Blow as hard as you can. This forces air around the egg and into the bottle. When you stop blowing, the increased air pressure behind the egg forces it out of the bottle.

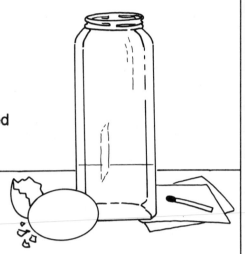

**Materials Needed:** (* Indicates student worksheet answers)

1. Student Scientific Method sheet
2. Individual Student Predictor
3. Classroom graph

* 4. Bottle containing a hard-boiled egg

**Teaching Procedure:**

1. Show students materials to be used in the experiment and state the problem.
2. Pass out individual student predictors and method sheet. Students mark their hypothesis.
3. Chart all student predictions on a class graph. Ask volunteers to explain the reasons for their predictions.
4. Discuss the graph with the class focusing on mathematical concepts.
5. Conduct the experiment. (See "Procedure" on the Scientific Method sheet.)
6. Discuss results as explained in the objective.
7. Have the class complete the student Scientific Method sheet.

**Try this for fun:**

Try different-sized bottles and eggs. Good luck!

**Example of a classroom graph:**

Fold a piece of butcher paper in half and sketch the outline. Cut it out. Plain tag may be used for a simple pictograph.

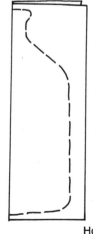
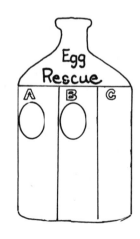

Name: _____

## Scientific Method
## Egg Rescue

**Problem:** How can we get the hard-boiled egg out of the bottle without breaking the egg or the bottle?

**Collect Materials:**

1. _____

**Hypothesis:** The egg will plop out after _____ .

> A. I blow into the bottle
> B. I shake the bottle
> C. I tap on the end

**Procedure:** Take the bottle containing an egg. Wash all the burned pieces of paper out of the bottle. Now try to get the egg out of the bottle. Good luck!

**Conclusion:** The egg plopped out after _____

_____

Draw a picture of our experiment:

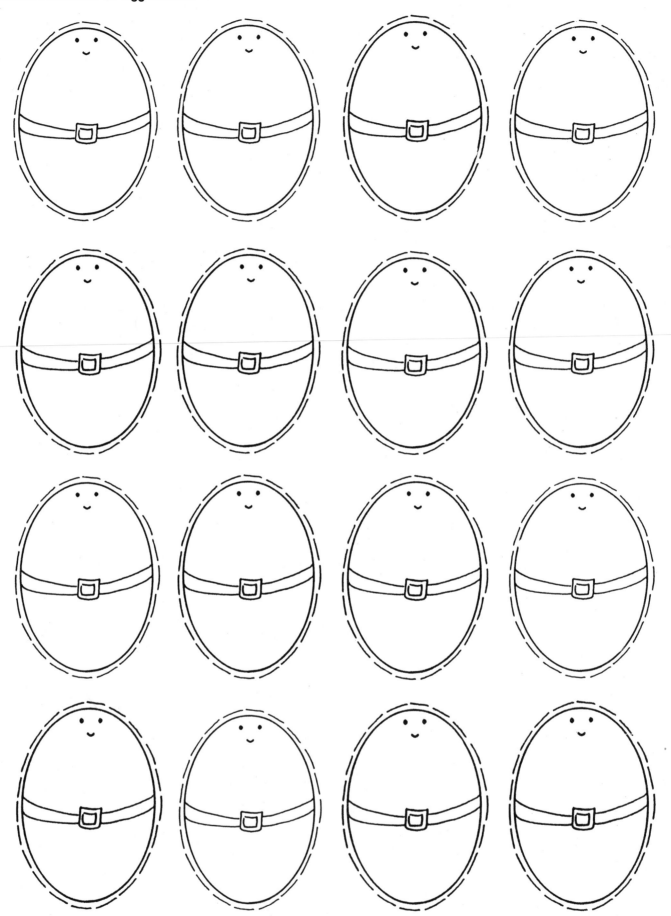

How to Do Experiments with Children

# Paper Magic

## Teacher Information Sheet

**Objective:** To teach that air has weight and exerts pressure

**Problem:** What will happen to a piece of paper when a ruler is placed under it and then hit by your hand?

The ruler will be held to the table because the weight of the air pressing down on the paper resists being pushed up suddenly. If you hit the ruler too hard, it could break, and the paper will not even be ripped!

**Materials Needed:** (* Indicates student worksheet answers)

1. Student Scientific Method Sheet
2. Individual Student Predictor
3. Classroom graph
* 4. Paper
* 5. Ruler

**Teaching Procedure:**

1. Show students materials to be used in the experiment and state the problem.
2. Pass out individual student predictors and method sheet. Students mark their hypothesis.
3. Chart all student predictions on a class graph. Ask volunteers to explain the reasons for their predictions.
4. Discuss the graph with the class focusing on mathematical concepts.
5. Conduct the experiment. (See "Procedure" on the Scientific Method sheet.)
6. Discuss results as explained in the objective.
7. Have the class complete the student Scientific Method sheet.

**Try this for fun:**

Try different weights of paper from newspaper to cardboard.

**Example of a classroom graph:**

Plain tag may be used for a simple pictograph.

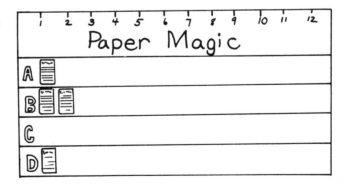

Name: _____

## Scientific Method
## Paper Magic

**Problem:** What will happen to a piece of paper when a ruler is placed under it and then hit by your hand?

**Collect Materials:**

1. _____

2. _____

**Hypothesis:** The piece of paper will _____ .

        A. fly up in the air
        B. tear apart
        C. fall to the ground
        D. hold the ruler down to the table

**Procedure:** Place a ruler on a table and cover it with a large piece of paper. Leave part of the ruler over the edge of the table and hit it with your hand. Watch carefully!

**Conclusion:** The paper _____

_____

Draw a picture of our experiment:

How to Do Experiments with Children

# Follow the Bouncing Ball
## Teacher Information Sheet

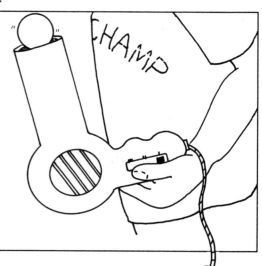

**Objective:** To teach that moving air exerts less pressure than still air

**Problem:** What will happen to a Ping Pong ball when the dryer is turned on?

When air is not moving, it pushes equally on objects from every direction. Rapidly moving air has a lower pressure. Air from the dryer moves faster around the sides of the ball than does the still air on top. Thus the ball seems to float above the dryer.

**Materials Needed:** (*Indicates student worksheet answers)

1. Student Scientific Method sheet
2. Individual Student Predictor
3. Classroom graph
* 4. Dryer
* 5. Ping Pong ball

**Teaching Procedure:**

1. Show students materials to be used in the experiment and state the problem.
2. Pass out individual student predictors and method sheet. Students mark their hypothesis.
3. Chart all student predictions on a class graph. Ask volunteers to explain the reasons for their predictions.
4. Discuss the graph with the class focusing on mathematical concepts.
5. Conduct the experiment. (See "Procedure" on the Scientific Method sheet.)
6. Discuss results as explained in the objective.
7. Have the class complete the student Scientific Method sheet.

**Try this for fun:**

Repeat the experiment using a heavier ball or try something light, such as confetti.

**Example of a classroom graph:**

Plain tag may be used for a simple pictograph.

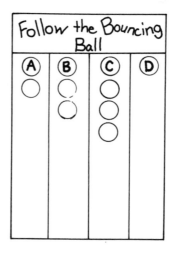

Name: _____

## Scientific Method
## Follow the Bouncing Ball

**Problem:** What will happen to a Ping Pong ball when the dryer is turned on?

**Collect Material:**

1. _____

2. _____

**Hypothesis:** The Ping Pong ball will_____ .

        A. blow away
        B. suspend in air
        C. break apart
        D. melt

**Procedure:** Put a Ping Pong ball on top of the blow dryer, which is facing up. Turn it on. Watch what happens.

**Conclusion:** The Ping Pong ball will_____

_____

Draw a picture of our experiment:

How to Do Experiments with Children

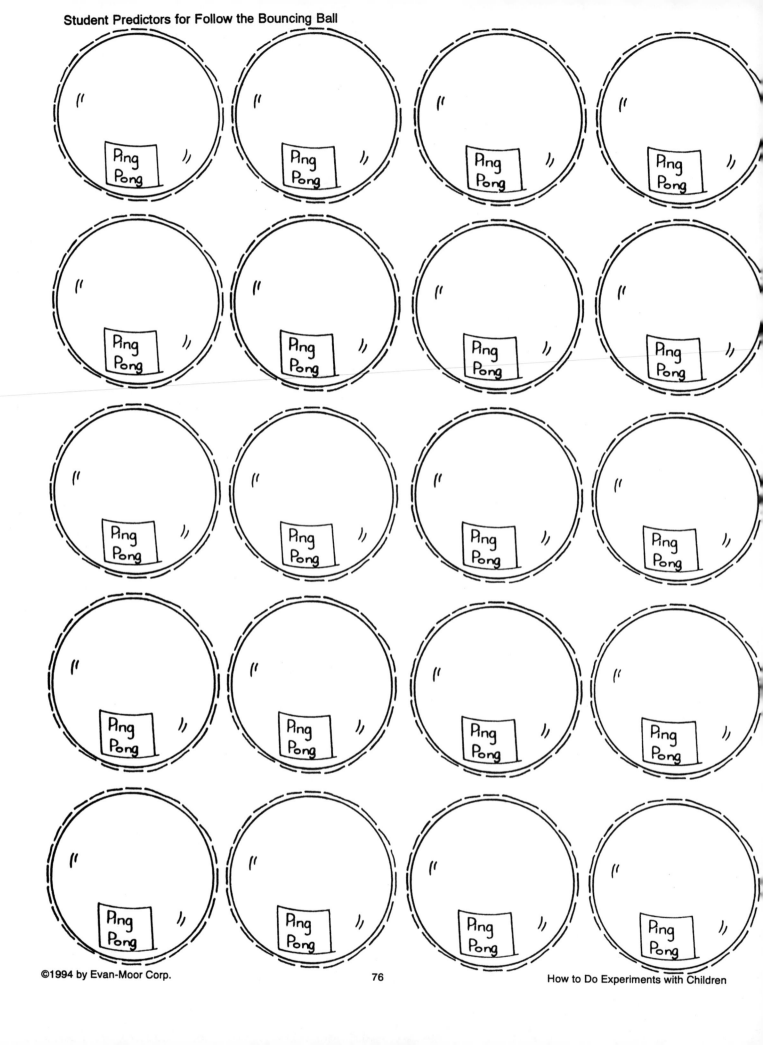

How to Do Experiments with Children

# Bottled Up
## Teacher Information Sheet

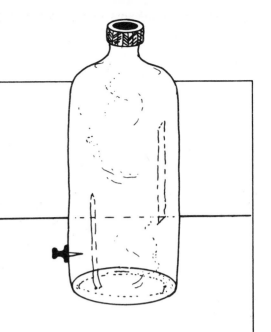

**Objective:** To teach that air pressure exerts a greater force than water pressure when the water is in a sealed container.

**Problem:** What will happen to the water in a plastic bottle when it is punctured with a push pin?

Air presses from outside the bottle and water presses from inside the bottle. The air pressure on the outside is stronger than the water pressure inside. Thus, the water is kept from pouring out of the small hole created when you pull the push pin out of the side of the bottle. (A plastic glue bottle works well.)

**Materials Needed:** (*Indicates student worksheet answers)

1. Student Scientific Method sheet
2. Individual Student Predictor
3. Classroom graph

* 4. Bottle
* 5. Water
* 6. Push pin

**Teaching Procedure:**

1. Show students materials to be used in the experiment and state the problem.
2. Pass out individual student predictors and method sheet. Students mark their hypothesis.
3. Chart all student predictions on a class graph. Ask volunteers to explain the reasons for their predictions.
4. Discuss the graph with the class focusing on mathematical concepts.
5. Conduct the experiment. (See "Procedure" on the Scientific Method sheet.)
6. Discuss results as explained in the objective.
7. Have the class complete the student Scientific Method sheet.

**Try this for fun:**

Repeat the experiment leaving the cap off the bottle. What happens?

**Example of a classroom graph:**

Fold a piece of butcher paper in half and sketch the outline. Cut it out. Plain tag can be used for a simple pictograph.

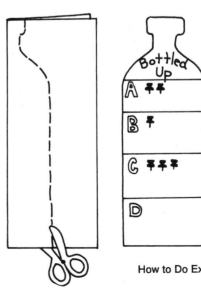

Name: _____

## Scientific Method
## Bottled Up

**Problem:** What will happen to the water in a plastic bottle when it is punctured with a push pin?

**Collect Materials:**

1. _____

2. _____

3. _____

**Hypothesis:** The water will _____ .

          A. stay inside
          B. squirt out
          C. pop the lid off
          D. make a hissing sound

**Procedure:** Poke a push pin into a plastic bottle. Fill the bottle with water and screw on the top. Now remove the push pin. Watch to see what happens to the water.

**Conclusion:** The water _____

_____

Draw a picture of our experiment:

How to Do Experiments with Children

# Tipsy
## Teacher Information Sheet

**Objective:** To teach that air exerts pressure on objects

**Problem:** What will happen when a glass filled with water has a piece of cardboard slid over the top and is then tipped over?

The cardboard used in this experiment will stay in place because of air pressure pushing up from the outside. This pressure is greater than the weight of the water pushing down on the cardboard from the inside. This experiment will work until the cardboard gets soggy. Make sure you hold the cardboard firmly when you turn the glass upside down. Try it over the sink first.

**Materials Needed:** (*Indicates student worksheet answers)

1. Student Scientific Method sheet
2. Individual Student Predictor
3. Classroom graph
* 4. Glass
* 5. Water
* 6. Cardboard

**Teaching Procedure:**

1. Show students materials to be used in the experiment and state the problem.
2. Pass out individual student predictors and method sheet. Students mark their hypothesis.
3. Chart all student predictions on a class graph. Ask volunteers to explain the reasons for their predictions.
4. Discuss the graph with the class focusing on mathematical concepts.
5. Conduct the experiment. (See "Procedure" on the Scientific Method sheet.)
6. Discuss results as explained in the objective.
7. Have the class complete the student Scientific Method sheet.

**Try this for fun:**

Try different weights of cardboard and/or paper.

**Example of a classroom graph:**

Fold a piece of butcher paper in half and sketch the outline. Cut it out. Plain tag can be used for a simple pictograph.

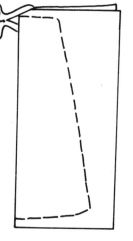

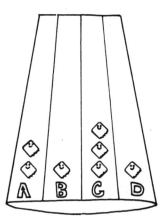

Name: _____

# Scientific Method
## Tipsy

**Problem:** What will happen when a glass filled with water has a piece of cardboard slid over the top and is then tipped over?

**Collect Materials:**

1. _____

2. _____

3. _____

**Hypothesis:** _____

        A.  The water will spill all over.
        B.  The water will sprinkle out slowly.
        C.  The cardboard will hold the water in the glass.
        D.  The water will change color.

**Procedure:** Fill a glass with water right to the top. Slide a piece of cardboard over the top of the glass. Hold the cardboard tightly and tip the glass over. Take your hand off of the cardboard. What happens?

**Conclusion:** _____

_____

Draw a picture of our experiment.

Student Projectors for Tipsy

How to Do Experiments with Children

# The Last Straw
## Teacher Information Sheet

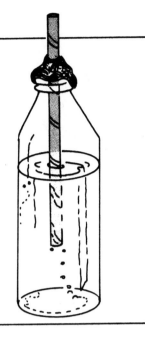

**Objective:** To teach that air moves from an area of high pressure to an area of low pressure

**Problem:** What will happen when you stop blowing through a straw which is sealed into a bottle of water?

Seal a straw into the mouth of a bottle with clay. Make sure it is a tight seal. (Florist's clay is waterproof and will form a better seal.) You should not be able to blow more than a few bubbles through the straw into the water. Blowing air into the bottle causes the pressure inside the bottle to be greater than the air pressure outside the bottle. When you remove your mouth, the compressed air expands and forces the water up the straw until the air pressure is back in balance. Stand back!

**Materials Needed:** (* Indicates student worksheet answers)

1. Student Scientific Method sheet
2. Individual Student Predictor
3. Classroom graph
*4. Bottle
*5. Water
*6. Straw
*7. Modeling clay

**Teaching Procedure:**

1. Show students materials to be used in the experiment and state the problem.
2. Pass out individual student predictors and method sheet. Students mark their hypothesis.
3. Chart all student predictions on a class graph. Ask volunteers to explain the reasons for their predictions.
4. Discuss the graph with the class focusing on mathematical concepts.
5. Conduct the experiment. (See "Procedure" on the Scientific Method sheet.)
6. Discuss results as explained in the objective.
7. Have the class complete the student Scientific Method sheet.

**Try this for fun:**

Try different sized bottles. The bigger the bottle, the more air is compressed and the higher the water will squirt.

**Example of a classroom graph:**

Fold a piece of butcher paper in half, and sketch the outline. Cut it out. Plain tag can be used for a simple pictograph.

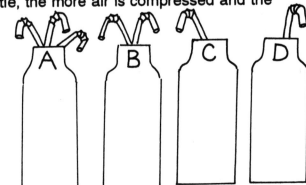

How to Do Experiments with Children

Name: _____

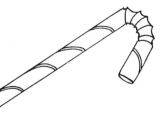

# Scientific Method
# The Last Straw

**Problem:** What will happen when you stop blowing through a straw which is sealed into a bottle of water?

**Collect Materials:**

1. _____    3. _____

2. _____    4. _____

**Hypothesis:** _____ .

        A.  The water will squirt out the top of the straw.
        B.  Nothing will happen.
        C.  Air pressure will blow the straw out of the bottle.
        D.  The straw will be pulled into the bottle.

**Procedure:** Fill a glass soda bottle three quarters full with water. Seal in the straw with modeling clay, making sure the straw is below the water surface. Hold the clay and blow through the straw.

**Conclusion:** _____

_____

Draw a picture of our experiment:

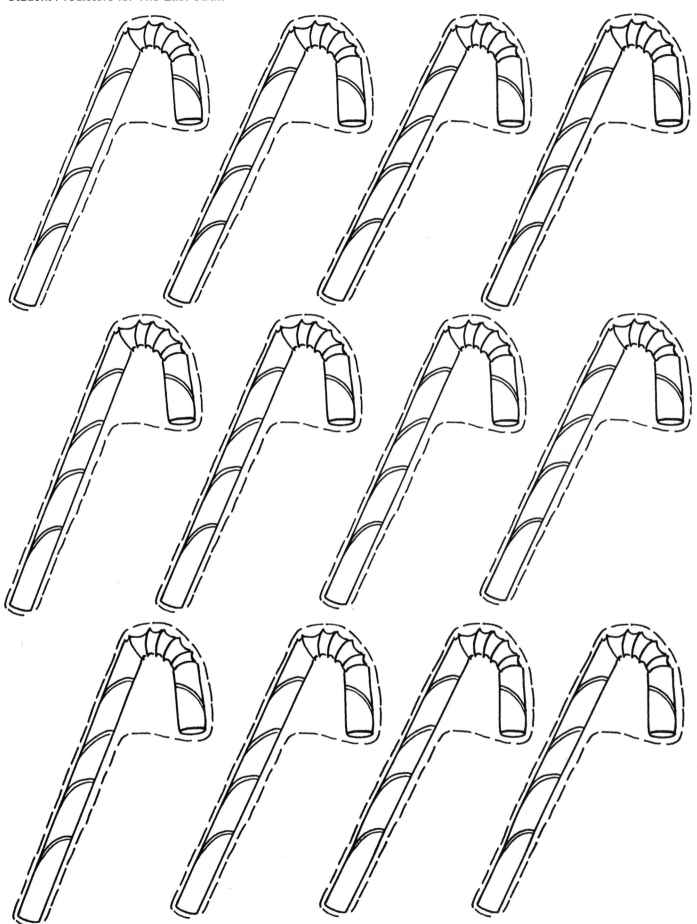

How to Do Experiments with Children

# Double Trouble
## Teacher Information Sheet

**Objective:** To teach that air moves from an area of high pressure to an area of low pressure

**Problem:** What will happen when you drink with two straws placed so that one straw is in the glass and the other straw is outside the glass?

When you suck on a straw you lower the pressure in your mouth. As atmospheric pressure pushes down on the liquid in the glass trying to equalize the pressure, liquid is pushed up the straw into your mouth. In this experiment the straw outside the glass of water will continue to bring air inside your mouth. This keeps the pressure the same both inside and outside your mouth. You will find it hard to drink any of the liquid.

**Materials Needed:**  (* Indicates student worksheet answers)

1. Student Scientific Method sheet
2. Individual Student Predictor
3. Classroom graph

*4. Glass
*5. Water
*6. Two straws

**Teaching Procedure:**

1. Show students materials to be used in the experiment and state the problem.
2. Pass out individual student predictors and method sheet. Students mark their hypothesis.
3. Chart all student predictions on a class graph. Ask volunteers to explain the reasons for their predictions.
4. Discuss the graph with the class focusing on mathematical concepts.
5. Conduct the experiment. (See "Procedure" on the Scientific Method sheet.)
6. Discuss results as explained in the objective.
7. Have the class complete the student Scientific Method sheet.

**Try this for fun:**

Try different lengths of straws. The longer the straw, the less water you get.

**Example of a classroom graph:**

Plain tag can be used for a simple pictograph.

Name: _____

## Scientific Method
## Double Trouble

**Problem:** What will happen when you drink with two straws placed so that one straw is in the glass and the other straw is outside the glass?

**Collect Materials:**

1. _____   3. _____

2. _____

**Hypothesis:** You can _____ .

        A. drink the water more quickly
        B. suck water in one and spit it out the other
        C. make bubbles as you drink
        D. hardly drink any of the water

**Procedure:** Place both straws in your mouth. Put the end of one in the glass of water and keep the other in the air. Now try drinking!

**Conclusion:** I _____

_____

Draw a picture of our experiment:

How to Do Experiments with Children

**Note:** This experiment needs to be demonstrated by the teacher since it involves the use of fire.

# The Water Mystery
## Teacher Information Sheet

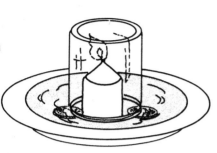

**Objective:** To teach that air moves from an area of greater pressure to an area of lesser pressure

**Problem:** What will happen to the colored water in the dish when the candle burns?

As the candle burns, the oxygen in the jar mixes with the carbon from the melted candle forming carbon dioxide. Removing the oxygen reduces the pressure in the jar. The greater air pressure outside the jar pushes the colored water up into the jar to fill the space left by the oxygen.

**Materials Needed:** (* Indicates student worksheet answers)

1. Student Scientific Method sheet
2. Individual Student Predictor
3. Classroom graph
*4. Candle
*5. Match

*6. Two coins
*7. Flat dish
*8. Water
*9. Jar
*10. Food coloring

## Teaching Procedure:

1. Show students materials to be used in the experiment and state the problem.
2. Pass out individual student predictors and method sheet. Students mark their hypothesis.
3. Chart all student predictions on a class graph. Ask volunteers to explain the reasons for their predictions.
4. Discuss the graph with the class focusing on mathematical concepts.
5. Conduct the experiment. (See "Procedure" on the Scientific Method sheet.)
6. Discuss results as explained in the objective.
7. Have the class complete the student Scientific Method sheet.

## Try this for fun:

Try different sized jars and check how much water rises in each jar.

## Example of a classroom graph:

Fold a piece of butcher paper in half, and sketch the outline. Cut it out. Plain tag can be used for a simple pictograph.

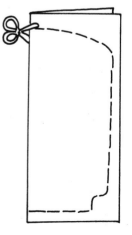

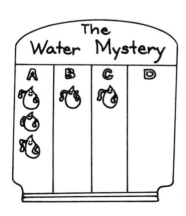

Name: _____

## Scientific Method
## The Water Mystery

**Problem:** What will happen to the colored water in the dish when the candle burns?

**Collect Materials:**

1. _____     5. _____

2. _____     6. _____

3. _____     7. _____

4. _____

**Hypothesis:** The water on the dish will _____ .

      A.  do nothing
      B.  bubble over
      C.  evaporate
      D.  be sucked into the jar

**Procedure:** Place two coins on a flat dish.  Cover the coins with water and place a candle in the center of the dish.  Light the candle and place the jar over it.  Be sure the jar sits on the two coins.  Observe what happens.

**Conclusion:** The water _____

Draw a picture of our experiment:

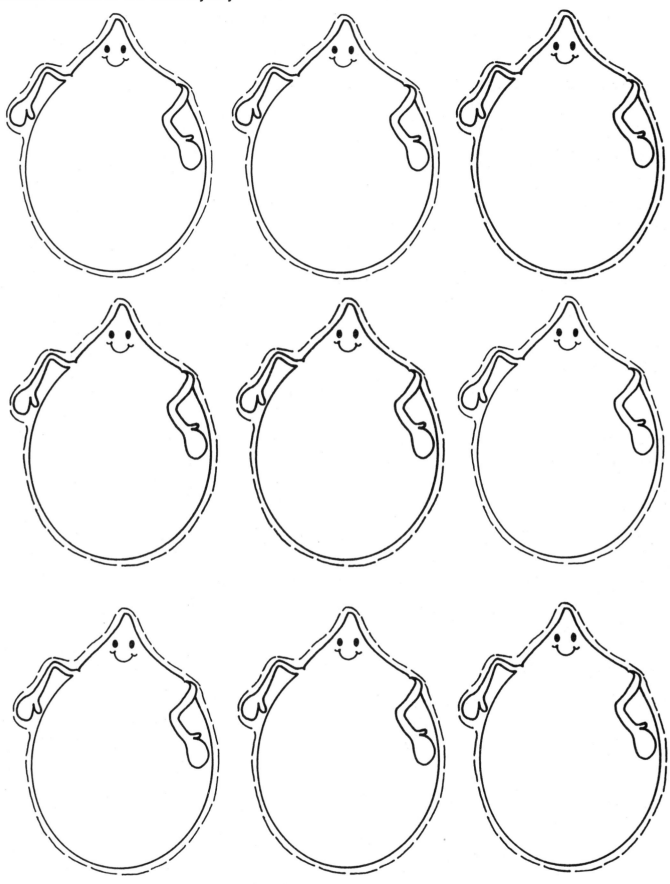

How to Do Experiments with Children

# Funnel Fun
## Teacher Information Sheet

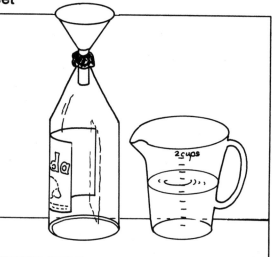

**Objective:** To teach a property of air pressure

**Problem:** What will happen to the water that is poured into a bottle through a funnel that is sealed onto the top of a bottle with clay?

A funnel is sealed into the top of a bottle with modeling clay. When water is poured quickly into the funnel, it compresses the air in the bottle below it. The air pressure in the bottle is greater than the air pressure outside the bottle. Therefore, the water will remain in the funnel.

**Materials Needed:** (* Indicates student worksheet answers)

1. Student Scientific Method sheet
2. Individual Student Predictor
3. Classroom graph
* 4. Funnel
* 5. Modeling clay
* 6. Water
* 7. Bottle

**Teaching Procedure:**

1. Show students materials to be used in the experiment and state the problem.
2. Pass out individual student predictors and method sheet. Students mark their hypothesis.
3. Chart all student predictions on a class graph. Ask volunteers to explain the reasons for their predictions.
4. Discuss the graph with the class focusing on mathematical concepts.
5. Conduct the experiment. (See "Procedure" on the Scientific Method sheet.)
6. Discuss results as explained in the objective.
7. Have the class complete the student Scientific Method sheet.

**Try this for fun:**

Try different-sized bottles and funnels. You may also vary the pouring rate of the water.

**Example of a classroom graph:**

Fold a piece of butcher paper in half and sketch the outline. Cut it out. Plain tag may be used for a simple pictograph.

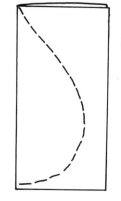

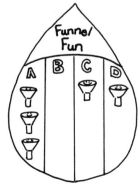

Name: _____

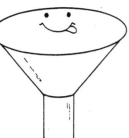

## Scientific Method
## Funnel Fun

**Problem:** What will happen to the water that is poured into a bottle through a funnel that is sealed onto the top of a bottle with clay?

**Collect Materials:**

1. _____     3. _____

2. _____     4. _____

**Hypothesis:** The water will _____ .

        A. stay in the funnel
        B. flow smoothly into the bottle
        C. enter the bottle in spurts
        D. dissolve the clay

**Procedure:** Seal a funnel onto the top of a bottle with clay. Pour water quickly into the funnel. Watch what happens!

**Conclusion:** The water _____

_____

Draw a picture of our experiment:

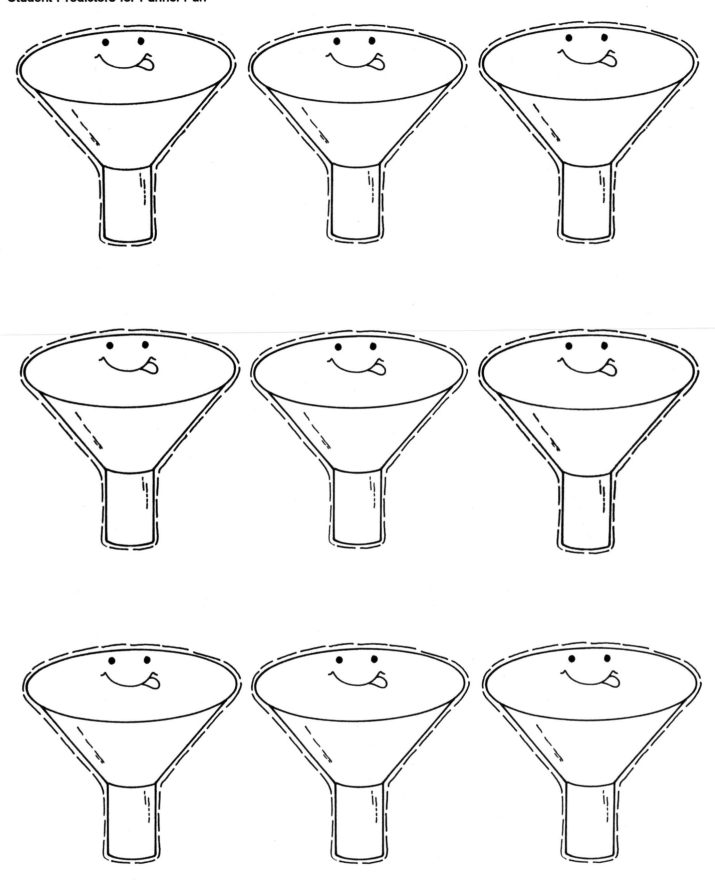

How to Do Experiments with Children

**Note:** This experiment must be demonstrated by the teacher as it uses hot water.

# Unbelievable Balloons
Teacher Information Sheet

**Objective:** To teach that warm air rises

**Problem:** What will happen to a balloon which has been stretched over the neck of a bottle when the bottle is placed in hot water?

When the hot water heats the air trapped in the bottle, the air will rise. The air will fill the balloon as it escapes from the bottle. Set the bottle in a bowl or sink of hot water.

**Materials Needed:** (* Indicates student worksheet answers)

1. Student Scientific Method Sheet
2. Individual Student Predictor
3. Classroom graph

    \* 4. Hot water
    \* 5. Bottle
    \* 6. Balloons

**Teaching Procedure:**

1. Show students materials to be used in the experiment and state the problem.
2. Pass out individual student predictors and method sheet. Students mark their hypothesis.
3. Chart all student predictions on a class graph. Ask volunteers to explain the reasons for their predictions.
4. Discuss the graph with the class focusing on mathematical concepts.
5. Conduct the experiment. (See "Procedure" on the Scientific Method sheet.)
6. Discuss results as explained in the objective.
7. Have the class complete the student Scientific Method sheet.

**Try this for fun:**

Use cold water. (No reaction will occur.)

**Example of a classroom graph:**

Make a chart on butcher paper or plain tag.

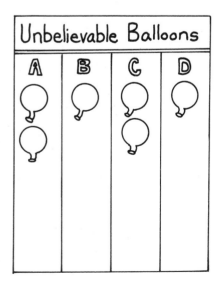

Name: _____

## Scientific Method
## Unbelievable Balloons

**Problem:** What will happen to a balloon which has been stretched over the neck of a bottle when the bottle is placed in hot water?

**Collect Materials:**

1. _____

2. _____

3. _____

**Hypothesis:** The balloon will _____ .

        A. burst
        B. fly off the top
        C. fill with air
        D. be sucked into the bottle

**Procedure:** Stretch a rubber balloon over the neck of an empty bottle. Put the bottle into hot water. Watch closely!

**Conclusion:** The balloon _____

_____

Draw a picture of our experiment:

Student Predictors for Unbelievable Balloons

# Eggstra-ordinary Experiment
### Teacher Information Sheet

**Objective:** To teach that air expands when heated and contracts when cooled

**Problem:** What will happen to a peeled hard-boiled egg when a lighted piece of paper is dropped into a bottle and the egg is placed over the opening of the bottle?

To have success with this experiment, a small egg just slightly larger than the mouth of the bottle works best. A little bit of cooking oil around the top of the bottle also helps. The gas inside the bottle expands as it is heated by the burning paper. Some of it is forced past the egg. After the fire goes out, the gas inside cools and contracts, forming a partial vacuum. The outside air pressure forces the egg down into the bottle.

**Materials Needed:** (*Indicates student worksheet answers)

1. Student Scientific Method sheet
2. Individual Student Predictor
3. Classroom graph
* 4. Bottle
* 5. Match
* 6. Paper
* 7. Hard-boiled egg (peeled)

## Teaching Procedure:

1. Show students materials to be used in the experiment and state the problem.
2. Pass out individual student predictors and method sheet. Students mark their hypothesis.
3. Chart all student predictions on a class graph. Ask volunteers to explain the reasons for their predictions.
4. Discuss the graph with the class focusing on mathematical concepts.
5. Conduct the experiment. (See "Procedure" on the Scientific Method sheet.)
6. Discuss results as explained in the objective.
7. Have the class complete the student Scientific Method sheet.

## Try this for fun:

Try different-sized eggs and different-sized bottles.

## Example of a classroom graph:

Fold a piece of butcher paper in half and sketch the outline. Cut it out. Plain tag may be used for a simple pictograph.

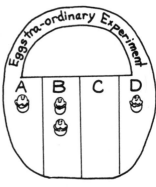
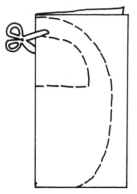

Name: _____

## Scientific Method
## Eggstra-ordinary

**Problem:** What will happen to a peeled hard-boiled egg when a lighted piece of paper is dropped into a bottle and the egg is placed over the opening of the bottle?

**Collect Materials:**

1. _____   3. _____

2. _____   4. _____

**Hypothesis:** The egg will _____ .

        A. be pushed into the bottle
        B. pop off
        C. begin to burn
        D. sit on top of the bottle

**Procedure:** Drop a burning piece of paper in a bottle and then place a peeled hard-boiled egg on the top. Watch out!

**Conclusion:** The egg _____

_____

Draw a picture of our experiment:

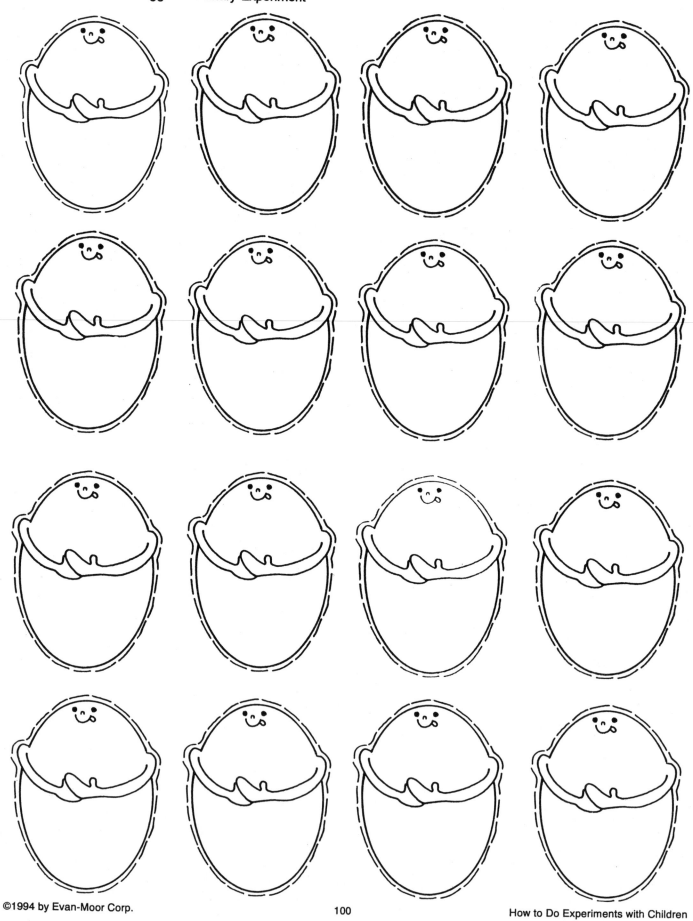

How to Do Experiments with Children

**Note:** This experiment must be demonstrated by the teacher since it uses hot water.

# Jug of Fun
## Teacher Information Sheet

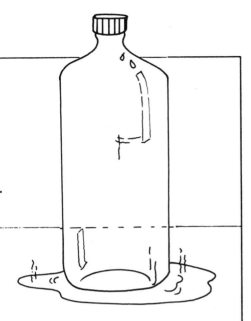

**Objective:** To teach that heat causes air to expand; cold causes air to contract

**Problem:** What will happen in a sealed bottle when the air is heated and then allowed to cool?

The hot water heats the air in the jug causing it to expand. Some of it escapes out of the top. When the water is emptied and the jug sealed, the air that is left starts to cool and contract. Because there is less air in the jug, it has less pressure than that on the outside. The outside pressure pushes the jug in. A plastic milk jug or a two-liter soft drink bottle works well. Be sure to screw on the cap immediately after emptying the water.

**Materials Needed:** (*Indicates student worksheet answers)

1. Student Scientific Method sheet
2. Individual Student Predictor
3. Classroom graph
* 4. Plastic jug
* 5. Hot water
* 6. Cap for jug

**Teaching Procedure:**

1. Show students materials to be used in the experiment and state the problem.
2. Pass out individual student predictors and method sheet. Students mark their hypothesis.
3. Chart all student predictions on a class graph. Ask volunteers to explain the reasons for their predictions.
4. Discuss the graph with the class focusing on mathematical concepts.
5. Conduct the experiment. (See "Procedure" on the Scientific Method sheet.)
6. Discuss results as explained in the objective.
7. Have the class complete the student Scientific Method sheet.

**Try this for fun:**

A metal can will also work. (Don't use a can that has contained anything flammable!) Pour I cup of water into a gallon can and heat until steam forms. Let it steam for about 5 minutes. Then remove it from the heat and immediately screw on the cap. You can speed the experiment along by pouring ice water on the can.

**Example of a classroom graph:**

Plain tag can be used for a simple pictograph.

| Jug of Fun | | | |
|---|---|---|---|
| A 👶 | | | |
| B 👶 👶 👶 | | | |
| C 👶 | | | |
| D | | | |

101  How to Do Experiments with Children

Name: _____

## Scientific Method
## Jug of Fun

**Problem:** What will happen in a sealed bottle when the air is heated and then allowed to cool?

**Collect Materials:**

1. _____

2. _____

3. _____

**Hypothesis:** The jug will _____ .

        A. collapse
        B. pop the cap off
        C. expand
        D. form condensation on the outside

**Procedure:** Fill a plastic jug half full of hot water and allow it to sit for one minute. Pour the water out, and immediately screw on the cap. Wait!

**Conclusion:** The jug _____

_____

Draw a picture of our experiment:

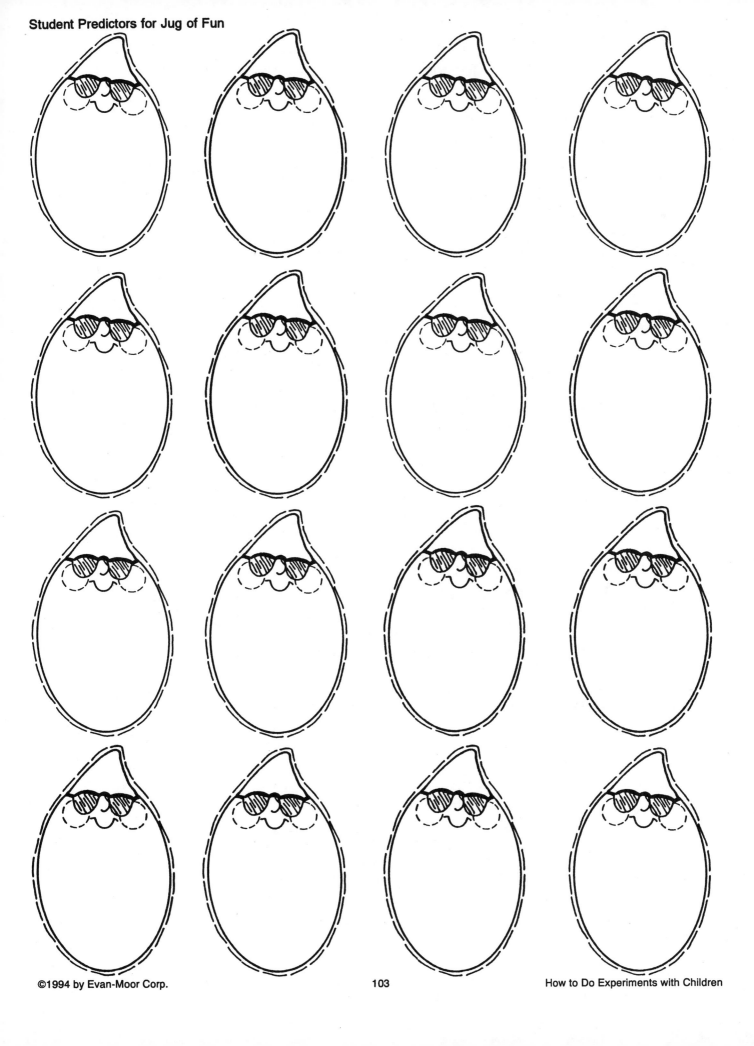

How to Do Experiments with Children

# It's Cold in Here!
## Teacher Information Sheet

**Objective:** To teach that cold air takes up less space than warm air.

**Problem:** What will happen to your balloon when it is placed in a refrigerator for a while?

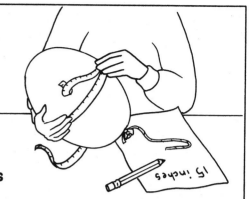

The speed at which molecules move is affected by temperature. Air contracts when it is cold and expands when it is warm. In this experiment the balloon decreases in size as it gets colder.

**Materials Needed:** (*indicates student worksheet answers)

1. Student Scientific Method sheet
2. Individual Student Predictor
3. Classroom graph
*4. Refrigerator (or ice chest)

*5. Balloon
*6. Paper and pencil
*7. Measuring tape
*8. String

**Teaching Procedure:**

1. Show students materials to be used in the experiment and state the problem.
2. Pass out individual student predictors and method sheet. Students mark their hypothesis.
3. Chart all student predictions on a class graph. Ask volunteers to explain the reasons for their predictions.
4. Discuss the graph with the class focusing on mathematical concepts.
5. Conduct the experiment. (See "Procedure" on the Scientific Method sheet.)
6. Discuss results as explained in the objective.
7. Have the class complete the student Scientific Method sheet.

**Try this for fun:**

Repeat the experiment putting one balloon in the freezer section and one balloon in the other part of the refrigerator.

**Example of a classroom graph:**

Plain tag may be used for a simple pictograph if desired.

| It's Cold in Here! | |
| --- | --- |
| A | |
| B | |
| C | |
| D | |

Name: _____

## Scientific Method
## It's Cold in Here!

**Problem:** What will happen to your balloon when it is placed in a refrigerator for a while?

**Collect Materials:**

1. _____     4. _____

2. _____     5. _____

3. _____

**Hypothesis:** The balloon will _____

        A.  pop
        B.  become larger
        C.  become smaller
        D.  not change

**Procedure:** Blow up the balloon and tie it shut with a piece of string. Measure the distance around the balloon. Write the number on your piece of paper. Put the balloon in a refrigerator. Leave it for at least an hour. Take the balloon out of the refrigerator and measure it again. Write this number on your sheet of paper. What happened to the balloon?

**Conclusion:** The balloon _____

_____

Draw a picture of our experiment:

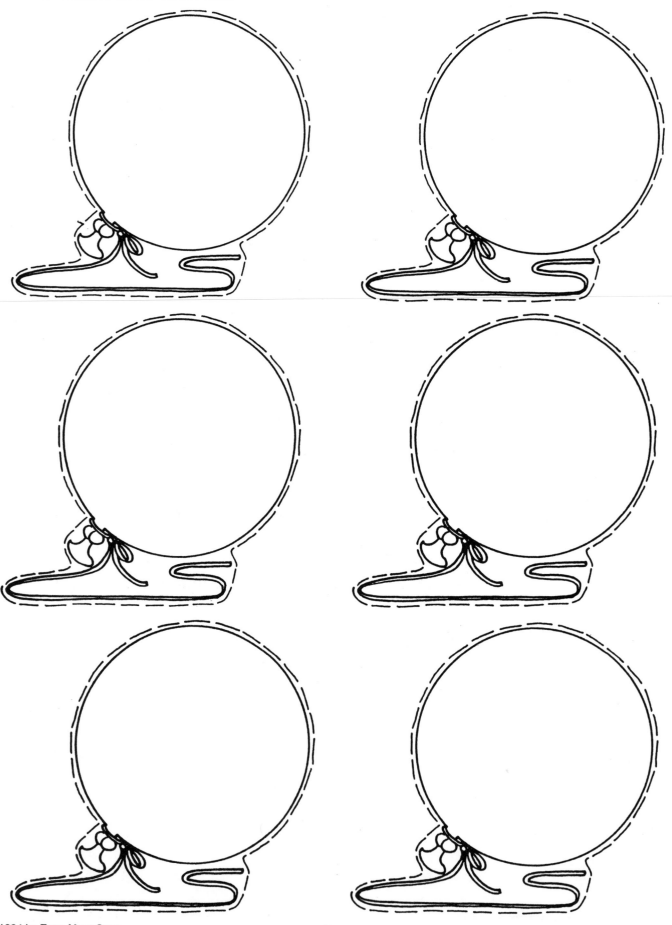

How to Do Experiments with Children

# A Real Cool Experiment

Teacher Information Sheet

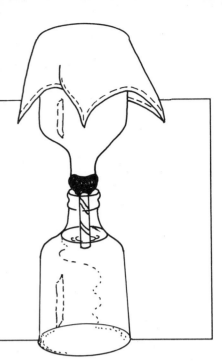

**Objective:** To teach that cold air contracts and occupies less space creating an area of lowered pressure

**Problem:** What will happen when a cold rag is placed on an inverted bottle?

Seal the straw into the top of the bottle with modeling clay. Place a very cold rag on top of the bottle. (See illustration.) The cold rag will make the air in the top bottle condense, thus creating a partial vacuum. The air pressure inside the bottom bottle forces the liquid up into the upper bottle which now has less air pressure in it.

**Materials Needed:** (* Indicates student worksheet answers)

1. Student Scientific Method Sheet
2. Individual Student Predictor
3. Classroom graph
* 4. Two bottles

* 5. Cold rag
  (soak in ice water)
* 6. Water

* 7. Straw
* 8. Modeling clay
* 9. Food coloring

**Teaching Procedure:**

1. Show students materials to be used in the experiment and state the problem.
2. Pass out individual student predictors and method sheet. Students mark their hypothesis.
3. Chart all student predictions on a class graph. Ask volunteers to explain the reasons for their predictions.
4. Discuss the graph with the class focusing on mathematical concepts.
5. Conduct the experiment. (See "Procedure" on the Scientific Method sheet.)
6. Discuss results as explained in the objective.
7. Have the class complete the student Scientific Method sheet.

**Try this for fun:**

Try a hot rag instead of a cold one.

**Example of a classroom graph:**

Plain tag can be used for a simple pictograph.

| A Real Cool Experiment | | |
|---|---|---|
| A | | |
| B | | |
| C | | |
| D | | |

How to Do Experiments with Children

Name: _____

# Scientific Method
## A Real Cool Experiment

**Problem:** What will happen when a cold rag is placed on an inverted bottle?

**Collect Materials:**

1. _____    4. _____

2. _____    5. _____

3. _____    6. _____

**Hypothesis:** The water in the bottle _____ .

        A. will bubble
        B. will come up the straw
        C. will do nothing
        D. will change color

**Procedure:** Seal a straw into a bottle. Invert the bottle and straw into another bottle filled with colored water. Now place a cold rag on top.

**Conclusion:** The water in the bottle _____

_____

Draw a picture of our experiment:

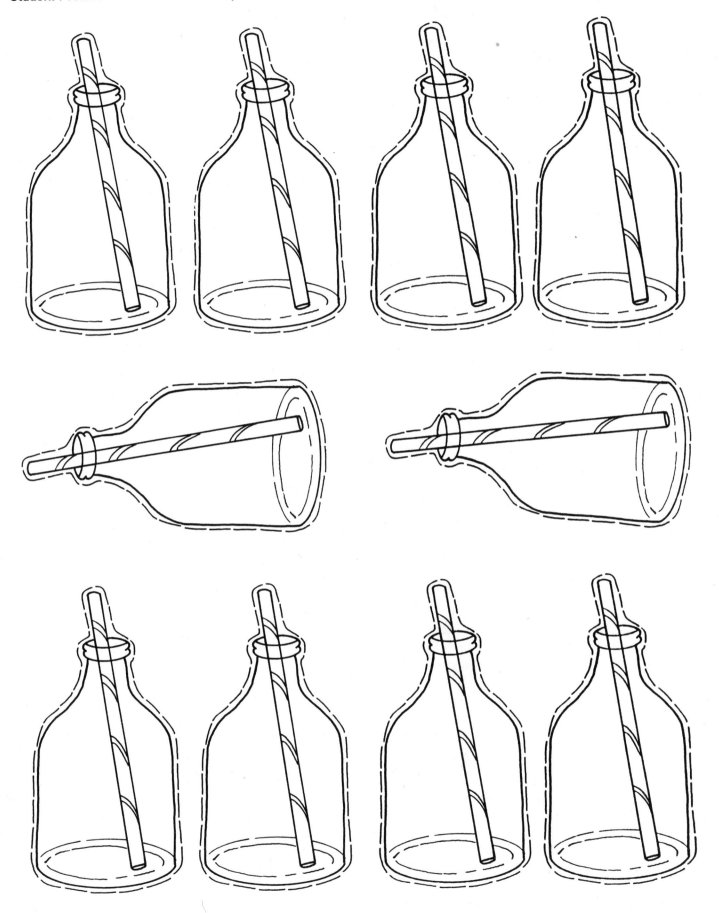

How to Do Experiments with Children

Note: This experiment will work with any copper coin.

# Bright as a New Penny
## Teacher Information Sheet

**Objective:** To teach that the two substances can combine to form a new substance.

**Problem:** What will happen to dull pennies when they are washed in a mixture of vinegar and salt?

The dull film on pennies forms when oxygen atoms from the air join the copper atoms in the pennies. Vinegar is acetic acid and table salt is sodium chloride. When the two are mixed together they form hydrochloric acid. The dull film on the pennies breaks down when the oxygen atoms in it join the atoms in the acid mixture leaving the pennies shining like new.

**Materials Needed:** (*indicates student worksheet answers)

1. Student Scientific Method sheet
2. Individual Student Predictor
3. Classroom graph
*4. Dull pennies
*5. Water

*6. White vinegar
*7. Salt
*8. Glass jar
*9. Measuring spoons
*10. Towel

**Teaching Procedure:**

1. Show students materials to be used in the experiment and state the problem.
2. Pass out individual student predictors and method sheet. Students mark their hypothesis.
3. Chart all student predictions on a class graph. Ask volunteers to explain the reasons for their predictions.
4. Discuss the graph with the class focusing on mathematical concepts.
5. Conduct the experiment. (See "Procedure" on the Scientific Method sheet.)
6. Discuss results as explained in the objective.
7. Have the class complete the student Scientific Method sheet.

**Try this for fun:**

Repeat the experiment using dirty silver coins.

**Example of a classroom graph:**

Plain tag may be used for a simple pictograph if desired.

| Bright as a New Penny | |
|---|---|
| A | 🪙🪙 |
| B | |
| C | 🪙 |
| D | 🪙 |

Name: _____

## Scientific Method
## Bright as a New Penny

**Problem:** What will happen to dull pennies when they are washed in a mixture of vinegar and salt?

**Collect Materials:**

1. _____    5. _____

2. _____    6. _____

3. _____    7. _____

4. _____

**Hypothesis:** The pennies will _____

        A. make a sizzling sound
        B. not change
        C. begin to bounce up and down
        D. become shiny

**Procedure:** Put some salt on one penny. Put some vinegar on one penny. See what happens. Now mix 6 tablespoons of vinegar and two tablespoons of salt in a jar. Put the dull pennies in the jar and stir them around for a few minutes. Rinse the pennies in water and dry them with a towel.

**Conclusion:** The mixture of salt and vinegar _____

_____

Draw a picture of our experiment:

112

**Note:** This experiment should be demonstrated by the teacher since it involves a "flying" cork.

# Cork Caper
## Teacher Information Sheet

**Objective:** To teach that two substances can be combined to create a gas

**Problem:** What will happen to the cork when baking soda and vinegar are mixed in the bottle?

Vinegar and baking soda produce carbon dioxide. The pressure produced by this gas will be enough to force the cork to fly off the top. Be sure to do this experiment **outside**! Use about 1 cup of vinegar and 1 to 2 tablespoons of baking soda. Wrap the baking soda in a tissue and drop it into the bottle. Use a plastic bottle if possible. There is less danger of breakage from the gas pressure. Point the cork end away from students.

**Materials Needed:** (* Indicates student worksheet answers)

1. Student Scientific Method sheet
2. Individual Student Predictor
3. Classroom graph
*4. Bottle
*5. Cork
*6. Vinegar
*7. Baking soda
*8. Tissue

**Teaching Procedure:**

1. Show students materials to be used in the experiment and state the problem.
2. Pass out individual student predictors and method sheet. Students mark their hypothesis.
3. Chart all student predictions on a class graph. Ask volunteers to explain the reasons for their predictions.
4. Discuss the graph with the class focusing on mathematical concepts.
5. Conduct the experiment. (See "Procedure" on the Scientific Method sheet.)
6. Discuss results as explained in the objective.
7. Have the class complete the student Scientific Method sheet.

**Try this for fun:**

Try using different sized bottles and different amounts of baking soda and vinegar.

**Example of a classroom graph:**

Plain tag can be used for a simple pictograph.

| Cork Caper | |
|---|---|
| A 🥤 | |
| B 🥤🥤 | |
| C 🥤 | |
| D 🥤 | |

How to Do Experiments with Children

Name: _____

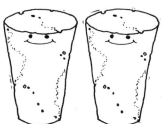

## Scientific Method
## Cork Caper

**Problem:** What will happen to the cork when baking soda and vinegar are mixed in the bottle?

**Collect Materials:**

1. _____     4. _____

2. _____     5. _____

3. _____

**Hypothesis:** The cork will _____ .

      A. be sucked into the bottle
      B. dissolve
      C. fly off
      D. change color

**Procedure:** Pour vinegar into a bottle. Wrap baking soda in a tissue. Drop it into the bottle. Place a cork in the top. Shake gently and watch what happens.

**Conclusion:** The cork _____

_____

Draw a picture of our experiment:

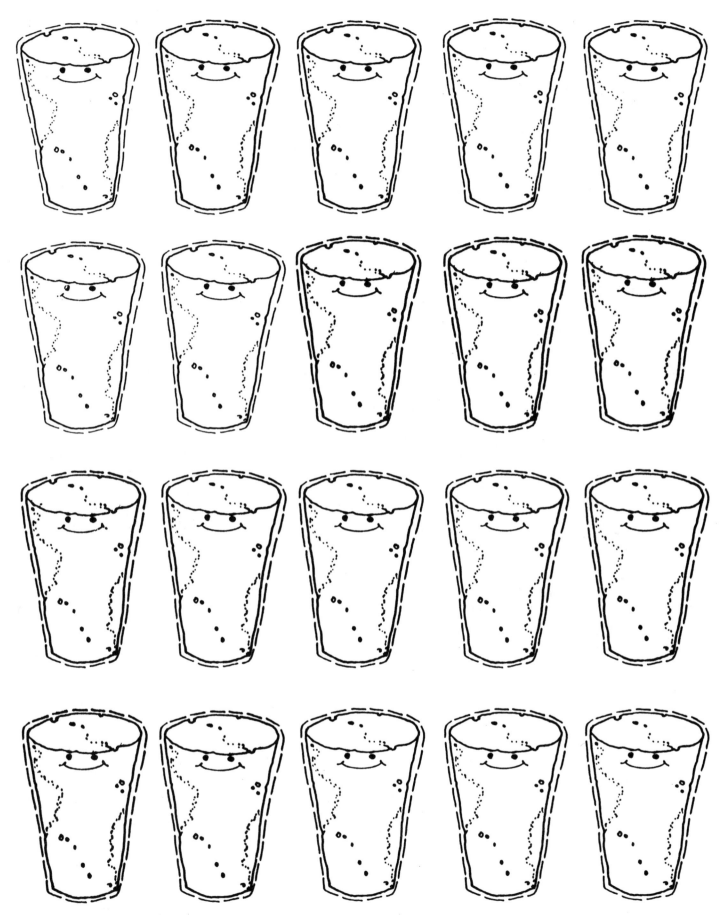

How to Do Experiments with Children

# The Big Balloon Take-Off
## Teacher Information Sheet

**Objective:** To teach that a gas is created when vinegar and baking soda are mixed

**Problem:** What will be in the balloon stretched over the neck of the bottle when you mix baking soda and vinegar in the bottle?

Vinegar and baking soda produce a gas (carbon dioxide) when mixed. The children will be able to see the gas trapped in the balloon. Be ready to put the balloon quickly over the top of the bottle. (You may extend this experiment by using the $CO_2$ in the balloon to extinguish the flame of a candle.)

**Materials Needed:** (* Indicates student worksheet answers)

1. Student Scientific Method Sheet
2. Individual Student Predictor
3. Classroom graph

* 4. Bottle
* 5. Balloons
* 6. Baking soda

* 7. Vinegar
* 8. Funnel
* 9. Tablespoon

## Teaching Procedure:

1. Show students materials to be used in the experiment and state the problem.
2. Pass out individual student predictors and method sheet. Students mark their hypothesis.
3. Chart all student predictions on a class graph. Ask volunteers to explain the reasons for their predictions.
4. Discuss the graph with the class focusing on mathematical concepts.
5. Conduct the experiment. (See "Procedure" on the Scientific Method sheet.)
6. Discuss results as explained in the objective.
7. Have the class complete the student Scientific Method sheet.

## Try this for fun:

Try different-sized balloons and bottles.

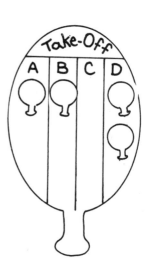

## Example of a classroom graph:

Fold a piece of butcher paper in half and sketch the outline of a balloon. Cut it out. Plain tag may be used for a simple pictograph.

Name: _____

## Scientific Method
## The Big Balloon Take-Off

**Problem:** What will be inside the balloon after you perform the experiment ?

**Collect Materials:**

1. _____   4. _____

2. _____   5. _____

3. _____   6. _____

**Hypothesis:** What do you think will happen? _____

       A. Nothing will happen.
       B. A loud explosion will happen.
       C. A gas called carbon dioxide will be made.
       D. A cloudy mixture will be made.

**Procedure:** Put 2 tablespoons of baking soda in a balloon. Put 8 tablespoons of vinegar in a bottle. Carefully stretch the end of the balloon over the top of the bottle. Mix vinegar and baking soda by tipping the baking soda out of the balloon into the bottle.

**Conclusions:** The balloon is full of _____

_____

Draw a picture of our experiment.

How to Do Experiments with Children

# Wooly Wonder
## Teacher Information Sheet

**Objective:** To teach that oxygen is used up during the rusting process

**Problem:** What will happen to a balloon when the steel wool begins to rust?

When steel wool rusts, it takes oxygen from the air and produces iron oxide. This reduces the pressure in the bottle and creates a suction that pulls the balloon into the bottle. Soaking the steel wool in vinegar removes its protective covering so it will rust. The drops of water help it to rust even faster. Leave the experiment alone for 24 hours in order to see the full effect.

**Materials Needed:** (* Indicates student worksheet answers)

1. Student Scientific Method sheet
2. Individual Student Predictor
3. Classroom graph

*4. Steel wool
*5. Water
*6. Balloon

*7. Bottle
*8. Vinegar
*9. Pencil
(to push wool into bottle)

## Teaching Procedure:

1. Show students materials to be used in the experiment and state the problem.
2. Pass out individual student predictors and method sheet. Students mark their hypothesis.
3. Chart all student predictions on a class graph. Ask volunteers to explain the reasons for their predictions.
4. Discuss the graph with the class focusing on mathematical concepts.
5. Conduct the experiment. (See "Procedure" on the Scientific Method sheet.)
6. Discuss results as explained in the objective.
7. Have the class complete the student Scientific Method sheet.

**Try this for fun:**

Try different shaped balloons.

**Example of a classroom graph:**

Fold a piece of butcher paper in half, and sketch the outline. Cut it out. Plain tag can be used for a simple pictograph.

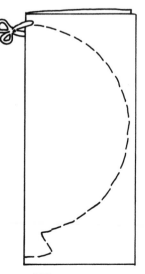

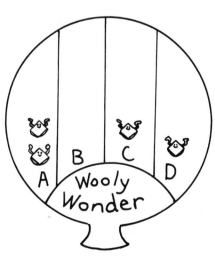

     How to Do Experiments with Children

Name: _____

## Scientific Method
## Wooly Wonder

**Problem:** What will happen to the balloon when the steel wool begins to rust?

**Collect Materials:**

1. _____     4. _____

2. _____     5. _____

3. _____     6. _____

**Hypothesis:** The balloon will _____ .

       A.  inflate on top of the bottle
       B.  fly off the top of the bottle
       C.  change color
       D.  turn inside out and inflate inside the bottle

**Procedure:** Push a piece of steel wool that has been soaked in vinegar into a glass bottle.  Put five drops of water into the bottle and stretch the balloon over the opening.  Now be patient and wait to see what happens.

**Conclusion:**  The balloon _____

_____

Draw a picture of our experiment:

How to Do Experiments with Children

**Note:** This experiment must be demonstrated by the teacher as it involves using sulfur and fire. It is best done in a well-ventilated room. Check with your principal before doing the experiment.

# Science in Full Bloom
## Teacher Information Sheet

**Objective:** To teach that a chemical reaction can cause a physical change

**Problem:** What will happen to a rose when it is exposed to burning sulfur and then dipped into hydrogen peroxide?

When sulphur burns, it produces the foul-smelling sulphur dioxide gas; this is what bleaches the flower. It takes oxygen from the colored part of the flower, changing it to white. The hydrogen peroxide puts the oxygen back and thus restores the color.

## Materials Needed:

1. Student Scientific Method Sheet
2. Individual Student Predictor
3. Classroom Graph
* 4. Rose
* 5. Glass

* 6. Sulphur
* 7. Foil and tape
* 8. Match
* 9. Hydrogen peroxide

## Teaching Procedure:

1. Show students materials to be used in the experiment and state the problem.
2. Pass out individual student predictors and method sheet. Students mark their hypothesis.
3. Chart all student predictions on a class graph. Ask volunteers to explain the reasons for their predictions.
4. Discuss the graph with the class focusing on mathematical concepts.
5. Conduct the experiment. (See "Procedure" on the Scientific Method sheet.)
6. Discuss results as explained in the objective.
7. Have the class complete the student Scientific Method sheet.

**Try this for fun:**

Try other flowers.

**Example of a classroom graph:**

Draw a picture on butcher paper. Plain tag may be used for a simple pictograph.

Science in Full Bloom

A 🌹

B 🌹 🌹

C 🌹

D 🌹 🌹

           How to Do Experiments with Children

Name: _____

# Scientific Method
# Science in Full Bloom

**Problem:** What will happen to a rose when it is exposed to burning sulphur and then dipped into hydrogen peroxide?

**Collect Materials:**

1. _____    4. _____

2. _____    5. _____

3. _____    6. _____

**Hypothesis:** The rose will _____ .

        A. wilt and die
        B. harden and crack into pieces
        C. be singed and then dissolve
        D. turn white, and then back to its original color

**Procedure:** Tape a rose to the inside of a glass. Burn sulphur on a piece of foil and place the glass upside down on top of it. Watch! Now take the rose and dip it in the hydrogen peroxide.

**Conclusion:** The rose _____

_____

Draw a picture of our experiment:

How to Do Experiments with Children

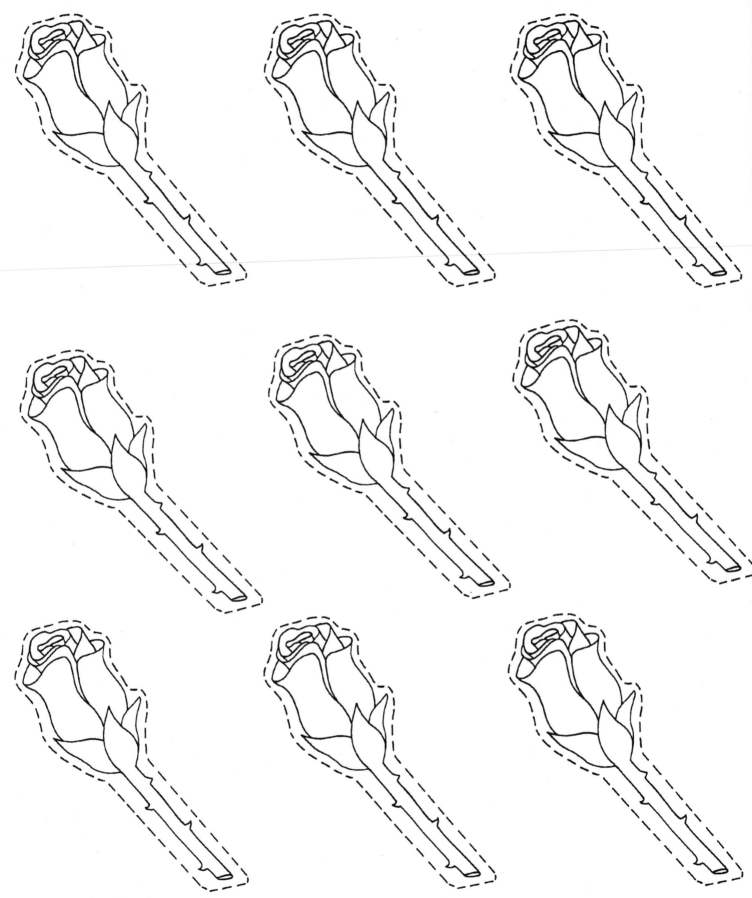

How to Do Experiments with Children

**Note:** You may want to save this experiment for Easter time.

# The Yolk's on You
### Teacher Information Sheet

**Objective:** To teach that an acid can dissolve some solids but not others

**Problem:** What will happen to a raw egg when it is soaked in vinegar for two days?

Vinegar, which is an acid, will cause the calcium in the egg shell to dissolve. The egg will appear to be rubbery in texture.

**Materials Needed:** (*Indicates student worksheet answers)

1. Student Scientific Method sheet
2. Individual Student Predictor
3. Classroom graph

* 4. An egg
* 5. A glass
* 6. Vinegar

**Teaching Procedure:**

1. Show students materials to be used in the experiment and state the problem.
2. Pass out individual student predictors and method sheet. Students mark their hypothesis.
3. Chart all student predictions on a class graph. Ask volunteers to explain the reasons for their predictions.
4. Discuss the graph with the class focusing on mathematical concepts.
5. Conduct the experiment. (See "Procedure" on the Scientific Method sheet.)
6. Discuss results as explained in the objective.
7. Have the class complete the student Scientific Method sheet.

**Try this for fun:**

At Thanksgiving, try a wishbone. This will require more time to appear rubbery.

**Example of a classroom graph:**

Fold a piece of butcher paper in half and sketch the outline of an Easter egg. Cut it out. Plain tag may be used for a simple pictograph.

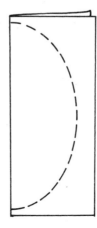

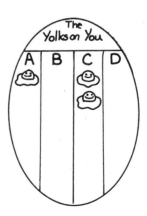

Name: _____

## Scientific Method
## The Yolk's on You

**Problem:** What will happen to a raw egg when it is soaked in vinegar for two days?

**Collect materials:**

1. _____

2. _____

3. _____

**Hypothesis:** The raw egg will _____ .

        A. become rubbery
        B. harden on the inside
        C. have its yolk disappear
        D. change color

**Procedure:** Place a raw egg in a glass. Fill the glass with enough vinegar to cover the egg. Let it sit for two days.

**Conclusion:** The egg will _____

_____

Draw a picture of our experiment

How to Do Experiments with Children

**Note:** Try this around Halloween. This experiment must be demonstrated by the teacher as it involves using fire and a sharp knife.

# Jack-O'-Light
Teacher Information Sheet

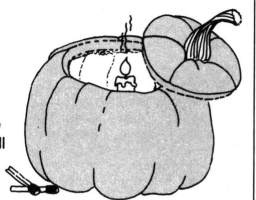

**Objective:** To teach that fire needs oxygen in order to burn

**Problem:** What will happen to the lighted candle inside the pumpkin when the pumpkin top is replaced?

Fire needs oxygen in order to burn. When the top of the pumpkin is replaced, the flame will extinguish because all of the oxygen is cut off. Do not cut the jack-o'-lantern until after the experiment. The larger the pumpkin, the longer the flame will burn.

**Materials Needed:** (* Indicates student worksheet answers)

1. Student Scientific Method Sheet
2. Individual Student Predictor
3. Classroom graph
* 4. Candle
* 5. Pumpkin
* 6. Match
* 7. Knife and spoon

## Teaching Procedure:

1. Show students materials to be used in the experiment and state the problem.
2. Pass out individual student predictors and method sheet. Students mark their hypothesis.
3. Chart all student predictions on a class graph. Ask volunteers to explain the reasons for their predictions.
4. Discuss the graph with the class focusing on mathematical concepts.
5. Conduct the experiment. (See "Procedure" on the Scientific Method sheet.)
6. Discuss results as explained in the objective.
7. Have the class complete the student Scientific Method sheet.

## Try this for fun:

Use various-sized pumpkins to compare the length of time needed for the flame to go out.

## Example of a classroom graph:

Fold a piece of butcher paper in half and sketch the outline of a jack-o'-lantern. Cut it out. Plain tag may be used for a simple pictograph.

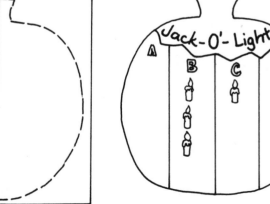

Name: _____

## Scientific Method
## Jack-O'-Light

**Problem:** What will happen to the lighted candle inside the pumpkin when the pumpkin top is replaced?

**Collected Materials:**

1. _____     3. _____

2. _____     4. _____

**Hypothesis:** The candle will _____ .

         A. burn up the pumpkin
         B. make the top pop off
         C. make the pumpkin shrivel up
         D. extinguish

**Procedure:** Scoop out a pumpkin. Place a lighted candle inside. Now put the top on. Wait and count to 60. Peek inside! What happened?

**Conclusion:** The candle _____

_____

Draw a picture of our experiment:

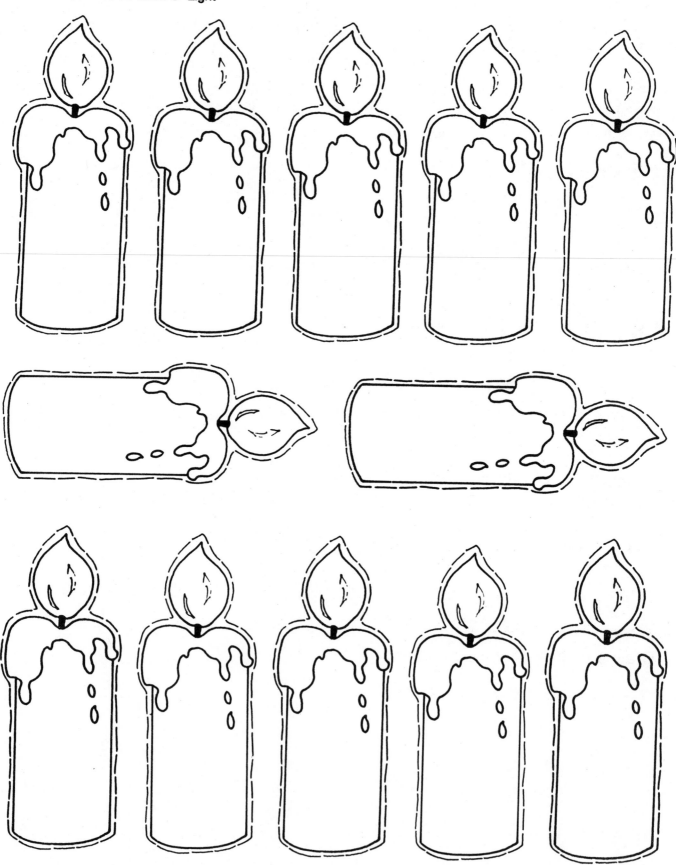

How to Do Experiments with Children

**Note:** Use around Hanukkah or Christmas. This experiment must be demonstrated by the teacher as it uses fire.

# Festival of Lights
## Teacher Information Sheet

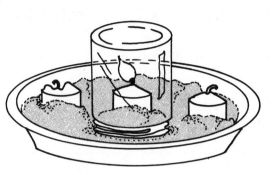

**Objective:** To teach that fire needs oxygen in order to burn

**Problem:** Which candle will burn longer?

Fire needs oxygen in order to burn. Using 3 different-sized jars will demonstrate which jar contains the most oxygen. Jar sizes such as baby food, pickle, and mayonnaise would work well. Fill a pie pan with sand and put a candle in the center. Sand provides a seal so no additional oxygen can get into the jar.

**Materials Needed:** (*Indicates student worksheet answers)

1. Student Scientific Method sheet
2. Individual Student Predictor
3. Classroom graph
* 4. Candle

* 5. Three jars
* 6. Stopwatch
* 7. Pie tin

* 8. Matches
* 9. Sand
* 10. Candle graph
   (page 48)

**Teaching Procedure:**

1. Show students materials to be used in the experiment and state the problem.
2. Pass out individual student predictors and method sheet. Students mark their hypothesis.
3. Chart all student predictions on a class graph. Ask volunteers to explain the reasons for their predictions.
4. Discuss the graph with the class focusing on mathematical concepts.
5. Conduct the experiment. (See "Procedure" on the Scientific Method sheet.)
6. Discuss results as explained in the objective.
7. Have the class complete the student Scientific Method sheet.

**Try this for fun:**

Try different-sized jars or glasses.

**Example of a classroom graph:**

Fold a piece of butcher paper in half and sketch the outline. Cut it out. Plain tag may be used for a simple pictograph.

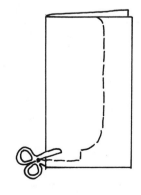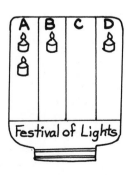

Name: _____

## Scientific Method
## Festival of Lights

**Problem:** Which candle will burn longer?

**Collect Materials:**

1. _____      4. _____

2. _____      5. _____

3. _____      6. _____

7. _____

**Hypothesis:** The candle in the _____ jar will burn longer.

        A. small
        B. medium
        C. large
        D. All burned the same length of time.

**Procedure:** Light the candle and place jar A over it. Use the stopwatch to find how long the candle will burn. Record the time on your Festival of Lights "candle" sheet. Repeat the same process with jars B and C.

**Conclusion:** The candle in _____ jar burned the longest because there was more oxygen.

Draw a picture of our experiment:

Student Predictors for Festival of Lights

**Note:** Reproduce this form for each child to use to record the results of the Festival of Lights experiment. Each candle represents one second. Children color the correct number of candles for each part of the experiment.

large **C**

medium **B**

small **A**

How many seconds will a candle burn under a jar?

How to Do Experiments with Children

**Note:** This should be demonstrated by the teacher or closely supervised by an adult since it involves using fire.

# Mystery Messages
### Teacher Information Sheet

**Objective:** To teach that heat can cause a chemical reaction to occur.

**Problem:** What will happen to your mystery message when the paper is heated over a candle?

In this experiment, heat causes the "invisible ink" to undergo a chemical reaction. The paper that has absorbed the lemon juice turns brown at a lower temperature than the rest of the paper so the message shows up. Have children write their messages using the round end of the toothpick.

**Materials Needed:** (*indicates student worksheet answers)

1. Student Scientific Method sheet
2. Individual Student Predictor
3. Classroom graph
*4. Paper
*5. Candle

*6. Candle holder
*7. Match
*8. Lemon juice
*9. Toothpicks

**Teaching Procedure:**

1. Show students materials to be used in the experiment and state the problem.
2. Pass out individual student predictors and method sheet. Students mark their hypothesis.
3. Chart all student predictions on a class graph. Ask volunteers to explain the reasons for their predictions.
4. Discuss the graph with the class focusing on mathematical concepts.
5. Conduct the experiment. (See "Procedure" on the Scientific Method sheet.)
6. Discuss results as explained in the objective.
7. Have the class complete the student Scientific Method sheet.

**Try this for fun:**

Repeat the experiment using milk or vinegar as your ink. Try other heat sources such as an iron or uncovered light bulb.

**Example of a classroom graph:**

Plain tag may be used for a simple pictograph.

Name: _____

## Scientific Method
## Mystery Messages

**Problem:** What will happen to your mystery message when the paper is heated over a candle?

**Collect Materials:**

1. _____    4. _____

2. _____    5. _____

3. _____    6. _____

**Hypothesis:** The message will _____

        A. stay a mystery
        B. mysteriously appear
        C. burn up

**Procedure:** Dip the toothpick in lemon juice. Write a mystery message on the piece of paper. Let the paper dry. Watch what happens to the message. Carefully warm the paper over a candle flame. Now what has happened?

**Conclusion:** The mystery message _____

_____

Draw a picture of our experiment:

**Note:** Teacher should demonstrate this activity as it involves fire and boiling water.

# Bubble and Boil
## Teacher Information Sheet

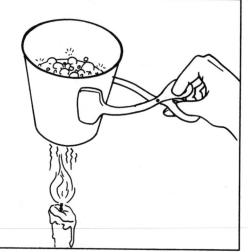

**Objective:** To teach that paper will not burn unless it can reach its kindling point.

**Problem:** What will happen to your cup of water when it is placed over a candle flame?

The water can reach the boiling point without the cup catching on fire because the water removes the heat so quickly that the paper cup never gets hot enough to ignite. You have oxygen and fuel present, but have removed the heat, the third element necessary for combustion to take place.

**Materials Needed:** (*indicates student worksheet answers)

1. Student Scientific Method sheet
2. Individual Student Predictor
3. Classroom graph
*4. Paper cup
*5. Candle

*6. Candle holder
*7. Match
*8. Water
*9. Tongs

**Teaching Procedure:**

1. Show students materials to be used in the experiment and state the problem.
2. Pass out individual student predictors and method sheet. Students mark their hypothesis.
3. Chart all student predictions on a class graph. Ask volunteers to explain the reasons for their predictions.
4. Discuss the graph with the class focusing on mathematical concepts.
5. Conduct the experiment. (See "Procedure" on the Scientific Method sheet.)
6. Discuss results as explained in the objective.
7. Have the class complete the student Scientific Method sheet.

**Try this for fun:**

Repeat the experiment using other nonflammable liquids to see if this makes a difference.

**Example of a classroom graph:**

Plain tag may be used for a simple pictograph if desired.

Name: _____

# Scientific Method
# Bubble and Boil

**Problem:** What will happen to your cup of water when it is placed over a candle flame?

**Collect Materials:**

1. _____    4. _____

2. _____    5. _____

3. _____    6. _____

**Hypothesis:** The cup of water will _____

        A. stay the same
        B. start to boil
        C. put the candle out
        D. catch fire

**Procedure:** Fill a paper cup half full of water. Light the candle. Hold the cup over the candle using tongs. Heat the water until it begins to boil. Watch what happens to the paper cup.

**Conclusion:** The paper cup _____

_____

Draw a picture of our experiment:

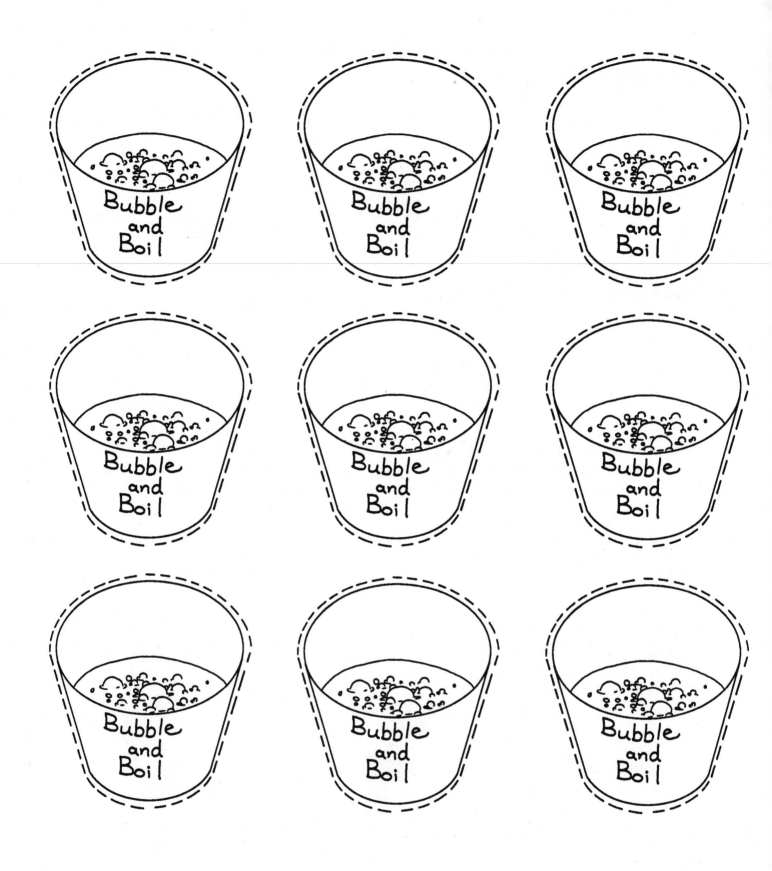

How to Do Experiments with Children

**Note:** This should be demonstrated by the teacher or closely supervised by an adult since it involves using fire.

# Hot Stuff
Teacher Information Sheet

**Objective:** To teach that heat travels through different materials at different speeds.

**Problem:** What will happen to a cloth wrapped around a quarter when a heated pencil is touched to it?

Wood is a poor conductor of heat. Metal is a good conductor of heat. In this experiment the quarter absorbs the heat from the hot pencil so quickly it moves through the cloth without any damage to the material. The cloth must be pulled very tightly around the coin for this to work.

**Materials Needed:** (*indicates student worksheet answers)

1. Student Scientific Method sheet
2. Individual Student Predictor
3. Classroom graph
*4. Pencil
*5. Candle

*6. Candle holder
*7. Match
*8. Quarter
*9. Piece of cotton cloth

**Teaching Procedure:**

1. Show students materials to be used in the experiment and state the problem.
2. Pass out individual student predictors and method sheet. Students mark their hypothesis.
3. Chart all student predictions on a class graph. Ask volunteers to explain the reasons for their predictions.
4. Discuss the graph with the class focusing on mathematical concepts.
5. Conduct the experiment. (See "Procedure" on the Scientific Method sheet.)
6. Discuss results as explained in the objective.
7. Have the class complete the student Scientific Method sheet.

**Try this for fun:**

Repeat the experiment using different types of cloth.

**Example of a classroom graph:**

Fold a piece of butcher paper in half and sketch the outline. Cut it out. Plain tag may be used for a simple pictograph.

Name: _____

## Scientific Method
## Hot Stuff

**Problem:** What will happen to a cloth wrapped around a quarter when a heated pencil is touched to it?

**Collect Materials:**

1. _____     4. _____

2. _____     5. _____

3. _____     6. _____

**Hypothesis:** The cloth will _____ .

        A. burn up
        B. do nothing
        C. drop the quarter
        D. smoke

**Procedure:** Wrap a quarter in a cloth tightly. Hold a pencil over a flame. Now place the point of the pencil on the cloth. Watch what happens.

**Conclusion:** The heat _____

_____

| Draw a picture of our experiment: |
| --- |
| |

How to Do Experiments with Children

# Mystery Brew
## Teacher Information Sheet

**Objective:** To teach that matter can change its form

**Problem:** What will happen when dry ice is placed in the Mystery Brew (water)?

Dry ice goes from solid form to gaseous form very quickly so you don't see the liquid state as you do when a regular ice cube melts. Be very careful when handling the dry ice in this experiment. You may want to wear kitchen oven mitts for extra protection.

**Materials Needed:** (*Indicates student worksheet answers)

1. Student Scientific Method sheet
2. Individual Student Predictor
3. Classroom graph

* 4. Tongs
* 5. Water
* 6. Dry ice
* 7. Cauldron (pot)

**Teaching Procedure:**

1. Show students materials to be used in the experiment and state the problem.
2. Pass out individual student predictors and method sheet. Students mark their hypothesis.
3. Chart all student predictions on a class graph. Ask volunteers to explain the reasons for their predictions.
4. Discuss the graph with the class focusing on mathematical concepts.
5. Conduct the experiment. (See "Procedure" on the Scientific Method sheet.)
6. Discuss results as explained in the objective.
7. Have the class complete the student Scientific Method sheet.

**Try this for fun:**

Try the recipe for Mystery Brew on page 147.

Place a regular ice cube in one saucer and a piece of dry ice in another saucer. Observe and compare what happens as they melt.

**Example of a classroom graph:**

Fold a piece of butcher paper in half and sketch the outline. Cut it out. Plain tag may be used for a simple pictograph.

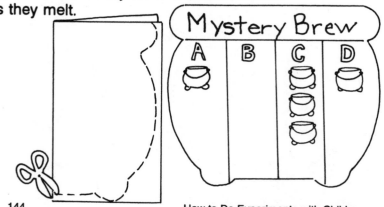

How to Do Experiments with Children

Name: _____

## Scientific Method
## Mystery Brew

**Problem:** What will happen when dry ice is placed in the Mystery Brew (water)?

**Collect Materials:**

1. _____     3. _____

2. _____     4. _____

**Hypothesis:** The Mystery Brew will_____.

       A. not change
       B. explode
       C. form a spooky fog
       D. change color

**Procedure:** Fill a cauldron with Mystery Brew (water). Using tongs, slowly lower the dry ice into the cauldron. Watch Out!

**Conclusion:** The Mystery Brew_____

_____

Draw a picture of our experiment:

How to Do Experiments with Children

# Mystery Brew

1/4 cup (.059 liter) Vampire Blood (cranberry juice or red Kool-aid)
1/2 cup (.118 liter) liquid star shine (7-up or Sprite)
1 scoop frozen swamp water (lime sherbet)
2 cat eyes (green grapes)
4 dried spiders (raisins)
3 goblin teeth (cloves)

Drink this tasty brew as you eat toad bones (pretzels) and rat brains (popcorn).

Add small chunks of dry ice for a fun time.

**Caution:** Be careful when handling dry ice. Always use tongs, not your fingers!

# Inka-Dinka-Do
## Teacher Information Sheet

**Objective:** To teach that the parts of a mixture can be separated and identified

**Problem:** Is purple ink always purple?

It is important in chemistry to detect unknown substances. When the water touches the dried ink it dissolves the molecules in the colors making up the ink. Different colors move farther allowing the ink to separate into rings of different colors. Use water-based ink or magic markers. Use absorbent paper such as coffee filters or paper towels. Place a drop of ink on the paper and hang it from a pencil resting across the top of the glass. Make sure the bottom of the paper, not the ink spot, touches the water.

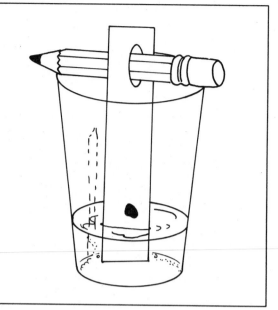

**Materials Needed:** (* Indicates student worksheet answers)

1. Student Scientific Method sheet
2. Individual Student Predictor
3. Classroom graph
*4. String
*5. Glass
*6. Purple ink
*7. Water
*8. Paper

## Teaching Procedure:

1. Show students materials to be used in the experiment and state the problem.
2. Pass out individual student predictors and method sheet. Students mark their hypothesis.
3. Chart all student predictions on a class graph. Ask volunteers to explain the reasons for their predictions.
4. Discuss the graph with the class focusing on mathematical concepts.
5. Conduct the experiment. (See "Procedure" on the Scientific Method sheet.)
6. Discuss results as explained in the objective.
7. Have the class complete the student Scientific Method sheet.

## Try this for fun:

Try different colors of ink. You may also want to experiment with permanent ink.

## Example of a classroom graph:

Plain tag can be used for a simple pictograph.

Name: _____

# Scientific Method
# Inka-Dinka-Do

**Problem:** Is purple ink always purple?

**Collect Materials:**

1. _____    4. _____

2. _____    5. _____

3. _____

**Hypothesis:** The purple ink will _____ .

           A. disappear
           B. separate into different colors
           C. stay the same color
           D. change the water to purple

**Procedure:** Cut a strip of paper towel and put a drop of ink at one end. Make a hole near the top of the other end and put a pencil through it. Set the strip over the cup with the water reaching the bottom of the towel. It should not touch the ink spot. Wait about 15 minutes.

**Conclusion:** The ink _____

_____

Draw a picture of our experiment:

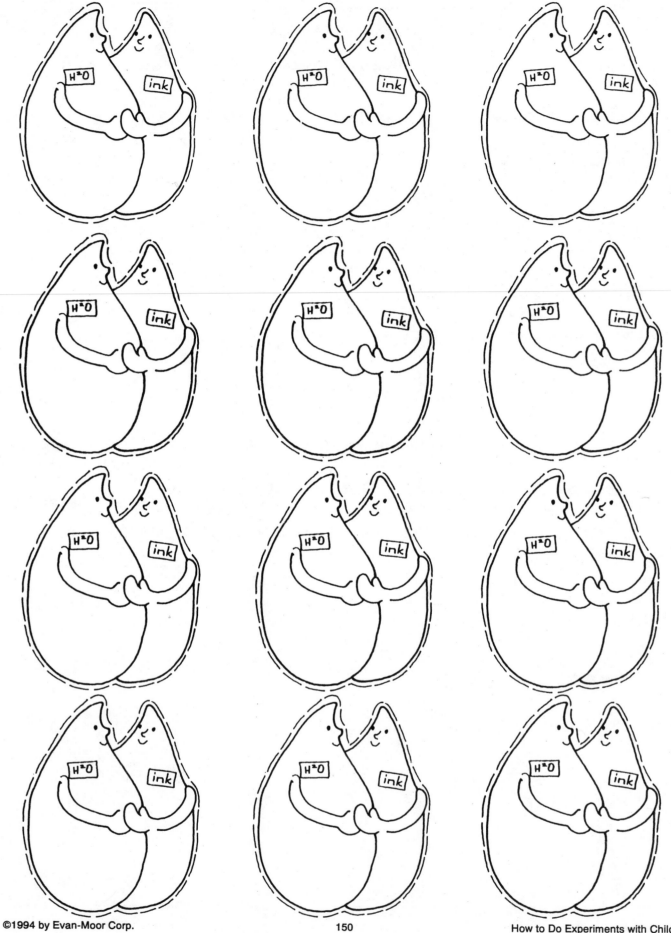

How to Do Experiments with Children

# Cool Cubes
## Teacher Information Sheet

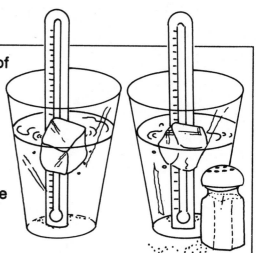

**Objective:** To teach that salt effects the freezing point of water

**Problem:** In which type of water (fresh or salt) will the ice cubes melt faster?

Fresh water freezes at 32 degrees F (at 0 degrees C). When salt is added to the water, the freezing temperature becomes lower than 32 degrees F. An ice cube in salt water will start to melt quickly because the ice cube is now warmer than the salty water.

**Materials Needed:** (*Indicates student worksheet answers)

1. Student Scientific Method sheet
2. Individual Student Predictor
3. Classroom graph

* 4. Two glasses
* 5. Water
* 6. Salt

* 7. Ice cube
* 8. Thermometer

## Teaching Procedure:

1. Show students materials to be used in the experiment and state the problem.
2. Pass out individual student predictors and method sheet. Students mark their hypothesis.
3. Chart all student predictions on a class graph. Ask volunteers to explain the reasons for their predictions.
4. Discuss the graph with the class focusing on mathematical concepts.
5. Conduct the experiment. (See "Procedure" on the Scientific Method sheet.)
6. Discuss results as explained in the objective.
7. Have the class complete the student Scientific Method sheet.

## Try this for fun:

Try adding household compounds, (e.g. baking soda, baking powder, etc.) to the water to see if they affect the melting rate.

## Example of a classroom graph:

Fold a piece of butcher paper in half and sketch the outline. Cut it out. Plain tag may be used for a simple pictograph.

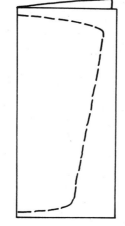

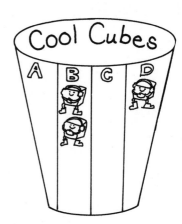

Name: _____

## Scientific Method
## Cool Cubes

**Problem:** In which type of water (fresh or salt) will the ice cubes melt faster?

**Collect Materials:**

1. _____    4. _____

2. _____    5. _____

3. _____

**Hypothesis:** Ice cubes _____ .

        A.  melt faster in fresh water
        B.  melt faster in salt water
        C.  melt at the same rate in fresh and salt water
        D.  will not melt

**Procedure:**  Fill two glasses -- one with salt water and one with fresh water.  Put an ice cube and a thermometer in each glass of water.  Wait and watch!

**Conclusion:**  Ice cubes _____

_____

Draw a picture of our experiment:

Student Predictors for Cool Cubes

How to Do Experiments with Children

# Presto Change-O
## Teacher Information Sheet

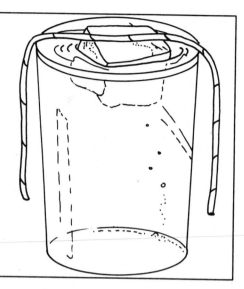

**Objective:** To teach that salt water freezes at a lower temperature than plain water

**Problem:** What will happen to string when salt is placed on the ice cube?

Water freezes at 32° F (0° C). When salt is sprinkled on the ice cube, it lowers the freezing point to below 32° F. Since the ice cube can't get any colder than it already is, the surface starts to melt. The string lies in the puddle of melted water. As the salt water is diluted by the melting ice cube, the freezing point rises. The water refreezes attaching the string to the ice cube.

**Materials Needed:** (* Indicates student worksheet answers)

1. Student Scientific Method sheet
2. Individual Student Predictor
3. Classroom graph

\* 4. Glass
\* 5. String
\* 6. Water

\*7. Ice cube
\*8. Salt

## Teaching Procedure:

1. Show students materials to be used in the experiment and state the problem.
2. Pass out individual student predictors and method sheet. Students mark their hypothesis.
3. Chart all student predictions on a class graph. Ask volunteers to explain the reasons for their predictions.
4. Discuss the graph with the class focusing on mathematical concepts.
5. Conduct the experiment. (See "Procedure" on the Scientific Method sheet.)
6. Discuss results as explained in the objective.
7. Have the class complete the student Scientific Method sheet.

## Try this for fun:

Try different types of thread or string of different weights.

## Example of a classroom graph:

Fold a piece of butcher paper in half and sketch the outline. Cut it out. Plain tag may be used for a simple pictograph.

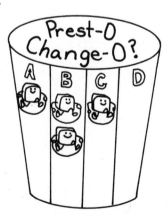

Name: _____

## Scientific Method
## Presto Change-O

**Problem:** What will happen to string when salt is placed on the ice cube?

**Collect Material:**

1. _____    4. _____

2. _____    5. _____

3. _____

**Hypothesis:** The ice cube and the string will _____ .

      A.  disappear
      B.  freeze together
      C.  do nothing
      D.  sink

**Procedure:** Lay the string across the top of an ice cube floating in a glass of water.  Sprinkle some salt on top and count to 10.  Presto! Watch what happens.

**Conclusion:** The ice cube and the string _____

_____

Draw a picture of our experiment:

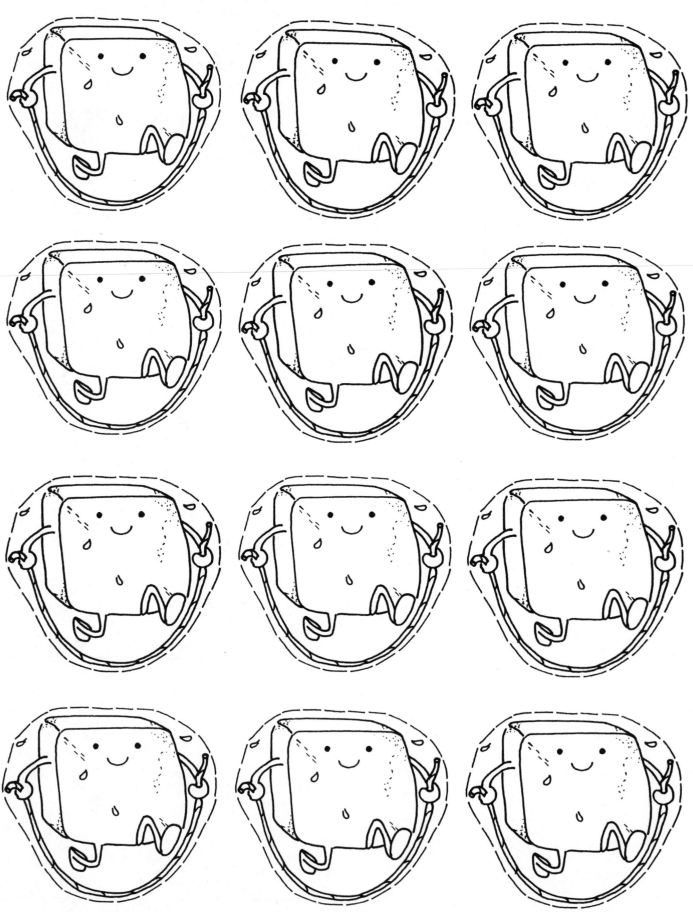

How to Do Experiments with Children

**Note:** This experiment must be demonstrated by the teacher as it involves using boiling water.

# Crazy Cubes
## Teacher Information Sheet

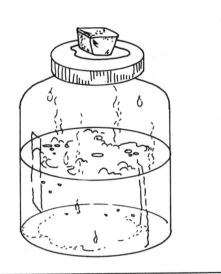

**Objective:** To teach that air pressure affects the boiling point of water

**Problem:** What will happen to water in a jar that has stopped boiling when an ice cube is placed on the lid?

Hot air rises. When boiling water in an open heat-proof glass jar, most of the air above the water heats up and leaves the jar. When the lid is placed on the jar, there is a little air and some water vapor left inside. Ice cubes on top of the lid cause the air below the lid to cool and make the water vapor condense. Because of the lower air pressure, the boiling point of the water is decreased, and it will begin to boil again.

**Materials Needed:** (*Indicates student worksheet answers)

1. Student Scientific Method sheet
2. Individual Student Predictor
3. Classroom graph
*4. Water
*5. Ice cubes

* 6. Hot pad or towel
* 7. Microwave oven or hot plate
   (Boil the water for one minute.)
* 8. Junior-sized baby food jar with
   a tight-fitting lid

## Teaching Procedure:

1. Show students materials to be used in the experiment and state the problem.
2. Pass out individual student predictors and method sheet. Students mark their hypothesis.
3. Chart all student predictions on a class graph. Ask volunteers to explain the reasons for their predictions.
4. Discuss the graph with the class focusing on mathematical concepts.
5. Conduct the experiment. (See "Procedure" on the Scientific Method sheet.)
6. Discuss results as explained in the objective.
7. Have the class complete the student Scientific Method sheet.

## Try this for fun:

Take the ice off and allow the water to stop boiling. Now replace the ice and the water will boil again. This may be repeated several times.

## Example of a classroom graph:

Fold a piece of butcher paper in half and sketch the outline of a jar. Cut it out. Plain tag can be used for a simple pictograph.

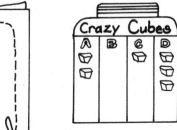

Name: _____

## Scientific Method
## Crazy Cubes

**Problem:** What will happen to the water (in a jar) that has stopped boiling when an ice cube is placed on the lid?

**Collect Materials:**

1. _____    4. _____

2. _____    5. _____

3. _____

**Hypothesis:** The water in the jar will _____ .

        A. freeze
        B. crack the jar
        C. evaporate
        D. begin to boil

**Procedure:** Fill a heat-proof jar 1/2 full of water. Bring the water to a boil. Let the water boil for one minute. Remove the jar carefully from the heat and place a lid on tightly. When the water stops boiling, place an ice cube on top of the lid. Watch what happens!

**Conclusion:** The water in the jar _____

_____

Draw a picture of our experiment:

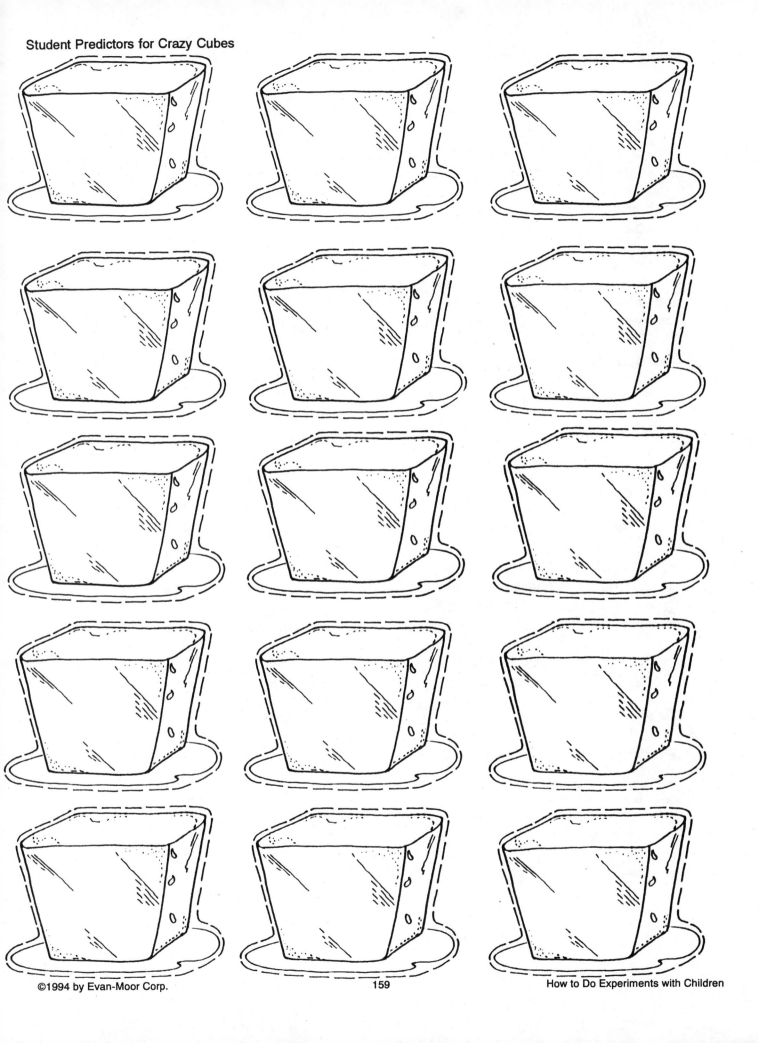

How to Do Experiments with Children

**Note:** This experiment must be demonstrated by the teacher as boiling water is being used.

# Soup's On
## Teacher Information Sheet

**Objective:** To teach that heat in the form of boiling water changes the form of certain foods

**Problem:** What happens to 3 different foods as they are added to boiling water?

When bouillon cubes are added to boiling water, they dissolve. Noodles soften and raw eggs congeal when added to boiling water. The students can try a little soup when it's done. Some even like it!

**Materials Needed:** (* Indicates student worksheet answers)

1. Student Scientific Method Sheet
2. Individual Student Predictor
3. Classroom graph
* 4. Bouillon cubes

* 5. Eggs
* 6. Noodles
* 7. Water

* 8. Spoon
* 9. Pot
* 10. Hot plate

**Teaching Procedure:**

1. Show students materials to be used in the experiment and state the problem.
2. Pass out individual student predictors and method sheet. Students mark their hypothesis.
3. Chart all student predictions on a class graph. Ask volunteers to explain the reasons for their predictions.
4. Discuss the graph with the class focusing on mathematical concepts.
5. Conduct the experiment. (See "Procedure" on the Scientific Method sheet.)
6. Discuss results as explained in the objective.
7. Have the class complete the student Scientific Method sheet.

**Try this for fun:**

Other ingredients could also be added.

**Example of a classroom graph:**

Plain tag may be used for a simple pictograph, if desired.

| ⟳ Soup's On ⟳ |
|---|
| A 🥣 |
| B 🥣 🥣 |
| C |
| D 🥣 |

Name: _____

# Scientific Method
## Soup's On

**Problem:** What happens to 3 different foods as they are added to boiling water?

**Collect Materials:**

1. _____    5. _____

2. _____    6. _____

3. _____    7. _____

4. _____

**Hypothesis:** The 3 different foods will _____ .

        A. stay the same
        B. change their form
        C. evaporate
        D. harden together

**Procedure:** Add these ingredients to a pot of boiling water: 2 bouillon cubes, 2 eggs (whipped), and a handful of thin noodles. Watch carefully and stir!

**Conclusion:** The three different foods _____

_____

Draw a picture of our experiment.

How to Do Experiments with Children

**Note:** You may want to save this experiment for Thanksgiving.

# Crazy Kernels
## Teacher Information Sheet

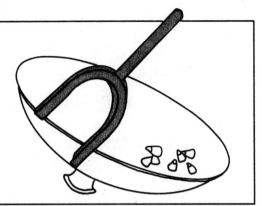

**Objective:** To teach that sound is created by vibration

**Problem:** What will happen to the popcorn kernels in a lid when the lid is touched with an active tuning fork?

Sound is made by vibrations. When the sound waves from the tuning fork hit the lid, the vibrations are transferred to the lid and then to the popcorn kernels. This causes the popcorn to "dance."

**Materials Needed:** (* Indicates student worksheet answers)

1. Student Scientific Method Sheet
2. Individual Student Predictor
3. Classroom graph

* 4. Tuning fork
* 5. Lid
* 6. Popcorn (unpopped)

**Teaching Procedure:**

1. Show students materials to be used in the experiment and state the problem.
2. Pass out individual student predictors and method sheet. Students mark their hypothesis.
3. Chart all student predictions on a class graph. Ask volunteers to explain the reasons for their predictions.
4. Discuss the graph with the class focusing on mathematical concepts.
5. Conduct the experiment. (See "Procedure" on the Scientific Method sheet.)
6. Discuss results as explained in the objective.
7. Have the class complete the student Scientific Method sheet.

**Try this for fun:**

Try to make other materials dance on the lid.

**Example of a classroom graph:**

Fold a piece of butcher paper in half and sketch the outline. Cut it out. Plain tag may be used for a simple pictograph.

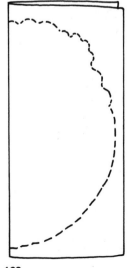

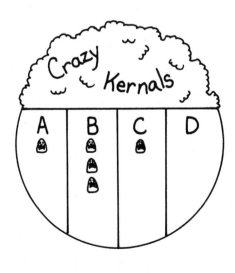

Name: _____

**Scientific Method**
**Crazy Kernels**

**Problem:** What will happen to the popcorn kernels in a lid when the lid is touched with an active tuning fork?

**Collect Materials:**

1. _____

2. _____

3. _____

**Hypothesis:** The popcorn kernels will _____ .

        A. dance
        B. do nothing
        C. pop
        D. spark

**Procedure:** Place popcorn kernels in a lid. Now hit a tuning fork and place it on the lid. Watch out!

**Conclusion:** The popcorn kernels _____

_____

Draw a picture of our experiment:

**Student Predictors for Crazy Kernels**

 How to Do Experiments with Children

# A Real Humdinger
## Teacher Information Sheet

**Objective:** To teach that sound is created by air passing over the vocal cords

**Problem:** How can you stop friends from humming without hurting them or their feelings?

While you are humming, air passes over your vocal cords creating a vibration. Pinching the nose closed, stops the air flow (if you are humming with your mouth closed). Thus, the vibration stops, as does the sound. In order for sound to exist, three properties must be present.

1. Something to produce vibrations
2. A medium for vibrations to travel
3. Something to receive the vibrations

**Materials Needed:** (*Indicates student worksheet answers)

1. Student Scientific Method sheet
2. Individual Student Predictor
3. Classroom graph

\* 4. Myself
\* 5. A friend

**Teaching Procedure:**

1. Show students materials to be used in the experiment and state the problem.
2. Pass out individual student predictors and method sheet. Students mark their hypothesis.
3. Chart all student predictions on a class graph. Ask volunteers to explain the reasons for their predictions.
4. Discuss the graph with the class focusing on mathematical concepts.
5. Conduct the experiment. (See "Procedure" on the Scientific Method sheet.)
6. Discuss results as explained in the objective.
7. Have the class complete the student Scientific Method sheet.

**Try this for fun:**

While humming, hold your hand against the front of your throat. What do you feel? Now pinch your nose. What happened?

**Example of classroom graph:**

Plain tag may be used for a simple pictograph, if desired.

| | | |
|---|---|---|
| A | ⊘ | |
| B | ⊘ | |
| C | | |
| D | ⊘ | ⊘ |

How to Do Experiments with Children

Name: _____

## Scientific Method
## A Real Humdinger

**Problem:** How can you stop a friend from humming without hurting him or his feelings?

**Collect Materials:**

1. _____

2. _____

**Hypothesis:** The humming stopped when _____ .

       A. I covered his eyes.
       B. I covered his mouth.
       C. I pinched his nose gently.
       D. I covered his ears

**Procedure:** Ask a friend to hum a song. His mouth must be kept closed while humming. Try all four choices. Which one worked?

**Conclusion:** The humming stopped when _____

_____

┌─────────────────────────────────────────────────────────────┐
│                                                               │
│ Draw a picture of our experiment.                             │
│                                                               │
│                                                               │
│                                                               │
│                                                               │
│                                                               │
│                                                               │
│                                                               │
│                                                               │
└─────────────────────────────────────────────────────────────┘

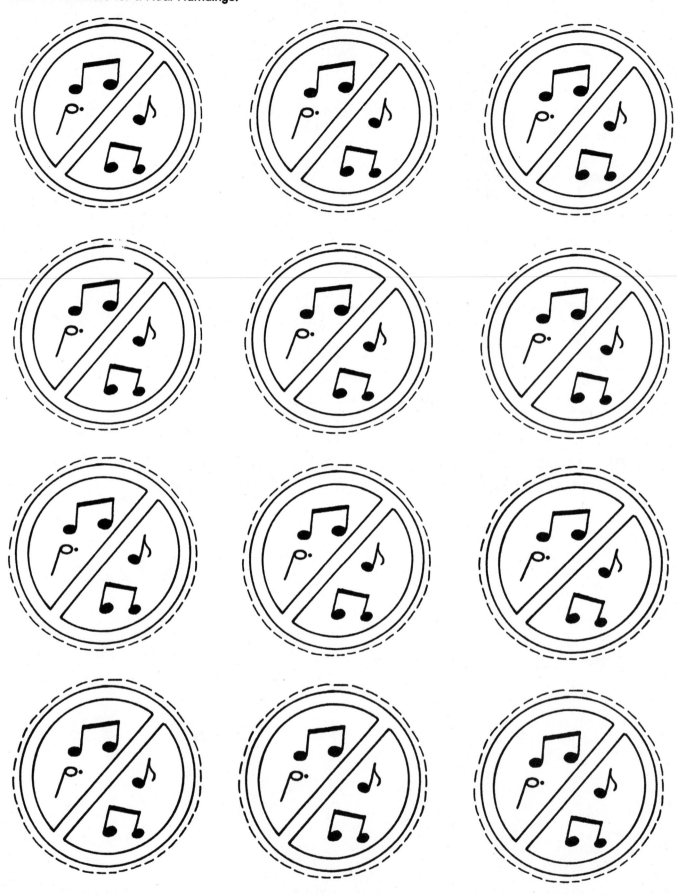

How to Do Experiments with Children

# A Sharp Experiment
## Teacher Information Sheet

**Objective:** To teach that sound vibrations travel through some mediums better than others

**Problem:** What will happen when you hold the end of a pencil with your teeth and scratch the other end?

Sound vibrations go through the wood of the pencil and through your teeth. Sound actually travels through some solid "mediums" better than through air because there are fewer things in the way to deflect the vibrations. In order for there to be sound, three things are necessary: 1) something to produce vibrations, 2) a medium for the vibrations to travel, and 3) something to receive the vibrations.

**Materials Needed:** (* Indicates student worksheet answers)

1. Student Scientific Method sheet
2. Individual Student Predictor
3. Classroom graph
*4. Pencil
*5. Your mouth

**Teaching Procedure:**

1. Show students materials to be used in the experiment and state the problem.
2. Pass out individual student predictors and method sheet. Students mark their hypothesis.
3. Chart all student predictions on a class graph. Ask volunteers to explain the reasons for their predictions.
4. Discuss the graph with the class focusing on mathematical concepts.
5. Conduct the experiment. (See "Procedure" on the Scientific Method sheet.)
6. Discuss results as explained in the objective.
7. Have the class complete the student Scientific Method sheet.

**Try this for fun:**

Try different materials or objects and see if you can still hear with your teeth.

**Example of a classroom graph:**

Plain tag can be used for a simple pictograph.

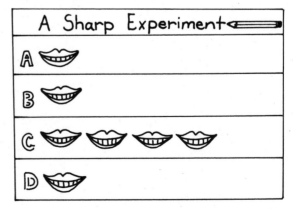

Name: _____

# Scientific Method
# A Sharp Experiment

**Problem:** What will happen when you hold the end of a pencil with your teeth and scratch the other end?

**Collect Materials:**

1. _____

2. _____

**Hypothesis:** You will _____ .

        A. drop the pencil
        B. hear with your teeth
        C. hear nothing
        D. get a toothache

**Procedure:** Take a pencil. Scratch one end with your fingernail. See what you hear. Now take the pencil and hold one end between your teeth. Scratch the other end and see what happens!

**Conclusion:** You _____

_____

Draw a picture of our experiment:

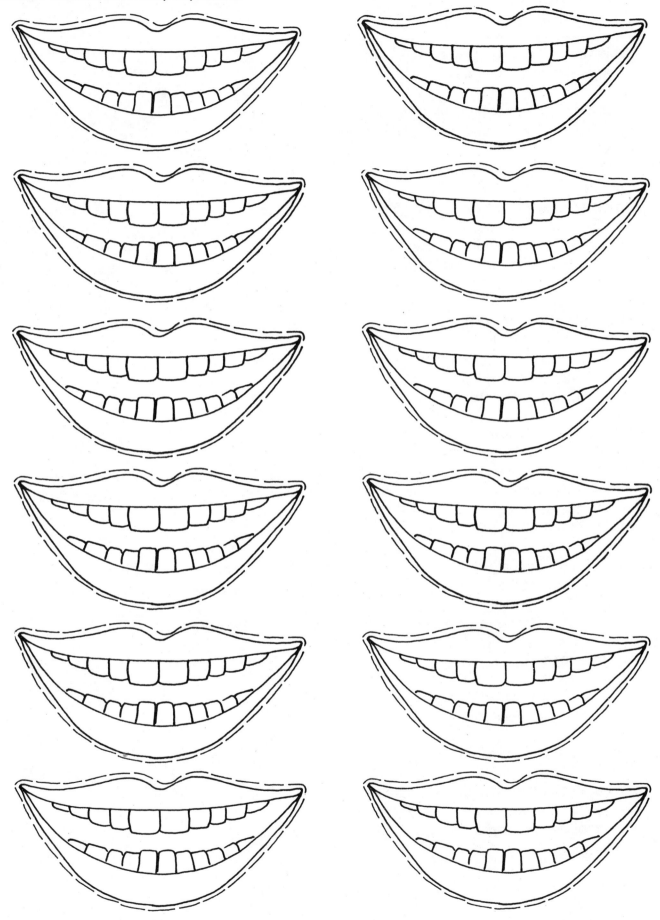

How to Do Experiments with Children

# Get a Charge Out of Science
## Teacher Information Sheet

**Objective:** To teach that an object with a static electric charge acts like a magnet

**Problem:** What will happen when a balloon rubbed on your hair is held above Styrofoam worms?

Rubbing a balloon on your hair rubs electrons off the hair and onto the balloon. This process makes the balloon negatively charged. The Styrofoam worms are positively charged and, thus, are attracted to the negatively charged balloon. *Be sure to try this experiment when the humidity is very low and the temperature is cold.*

**Materials Needed:** (* Indicates student worksheet answers)

1. Student Scientific Method sheet
2. Individual Student Predictor
3. Classroom graph

*4. Balloon
*5. Styrofoam worms
*6. Hair

**Teaching Procedure:**

1. Show students materials to be used in the experiment and state the problem.
2. Pass out individual student predictors and method sheet. Students mark their hypothesis.
3. Chart all student predictions on a class graph. Ask volunteers to explain the reasons for their predictions.
4. Discuss the graph with the class focusing on mathematical concepts.
5. Conduct the experiment. (See "Procedure" on the Scientific Method sheet.)
6. Discuss results as explained in the objective.
7. Have the class complete the student Scientific Method sheet.

**Try this for fun:**

Try different objects to see if they stick to the balloon: pieces of paper, Rice Krispies, etc.

**Example of a classroom graph:**

Fold a piece of butcher paper in half, and sketch the outline. Cut it out. Plain tag can be used for a simple pictograph.

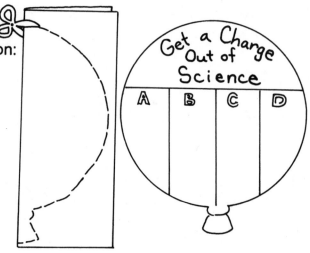

Name: _____

# Scientific Method
# Get a Charge Out of Science

**Problem:** What will happen when a balloon rubbed on your hair is held above Styrofoam worms?

**Collect Materials:**

1. _____    3. _____

2. _____

**Hypothesis:** The worms will _____ .

        A. wiggle around
        B. stick to the balloon
        C. stay still
        D. stick to each other

**Procedure:** Rub a balloon on your hair. Hold the charged balloon above the Styrofoam worms. Look out!

**Conclusion:** The worms _____

_____

```
Draw a picture of our experiment:




```

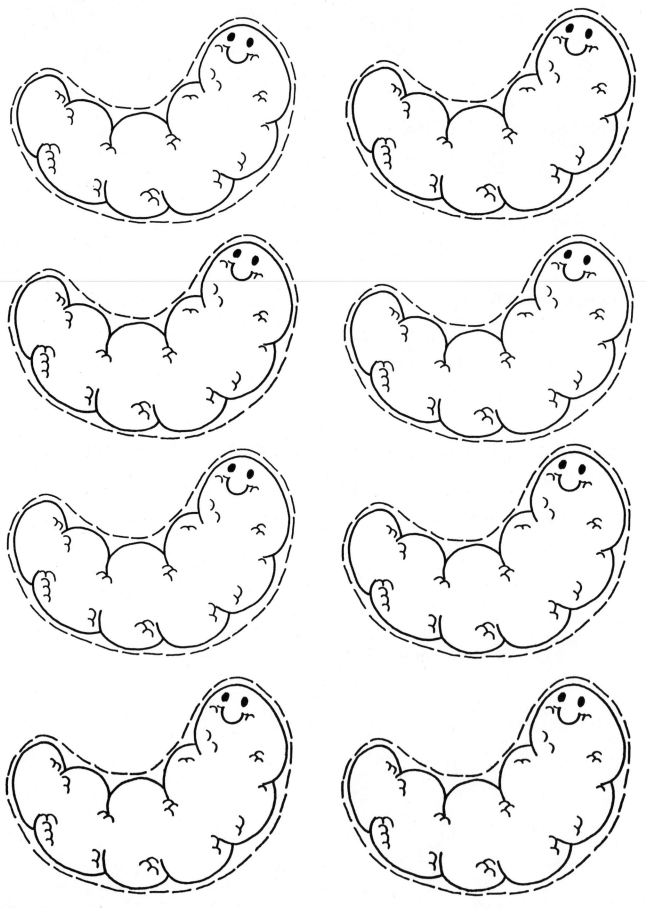

How to Do Experiments with Children

# Springtime Science
## Teacher Information Sheet

**Objective:** To teach that an object with a static electric charge acts like a magnet.

**Problem:** What will happen to the wings of a paper butterfly when a charged balloon is held near it and then moved away?

Draw a butterfly on tissue paper and glue its body to a piece of cardboard. When the body is dry, crease the wings so that they move freely up and down. Charge a balloon by rubbing it on your hair or a piece of wool and hold it near the wings. Now move the balloon away from the butterfly. As you move the balloon back and forth the wings will "flutter." The balloon has a negative charge but the paper has some positive atoms. The attraction of the positive and negative atoms is strong enough to defy the law of gravity.

**Materials Needed:** (* Indicates student worksheet answers)

1. Student Scientific Method Sheet
2. Individual Student Predictor
3. Classroom graph

* 4. Charged balloon
* 5. Paper butterfly

## Teaching Procedure:

1. Show students materials to be used in the experiment and state the problem.
2. Pass out individual student predictors and method sheet. Students mark their hypothesis.
3. Chart all student predictions on a class graph. Ask volunteers to explain the reasons for their predictions.
4. Discuss the graph with the class focusing on mathematical concepts.
5. Conduct the experiment. (See "Procedure" on the Scientific Method sheet.)
6. Discuss results as explained in the objective.
7. Have the class complete the student Scientific Method sheet.

## Try this for fun:

Try to produce the charge by rubbing the balloon on clothing. See what objects will be attracted to the balloon. Stick the balloon on the wall, make a student's hair rise, etc.

## Example of a classroom graph:

Fold a piece of butcher paper in half and sketch the outline. Cut it out. Plain tag may be used for a simple pictograph.

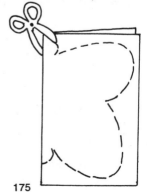

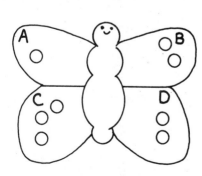

How to Do Experiments with Children

Name: _____

# Scientific Method
# Springtime Science

**Problem:** What will happen to the wings of a paper butterfly when a charged balloon is held near it and then moved away?

**Collect Materials:**

1. _____

2. _____

**Hypothesis:** The wings will _____ .

        A. stick to the cardboard
        B. make a humming sound
        C. flutter back and forth
        D. do nothing

**Procedure:** Charge an inflated balloon by rubbing it on your hair. Hold the charged balloon near the wings, then move it away. Watch carefully!

**Conclusion:** The wings _____

_____

Draw a picture of our experiment:

How to Do Experiments with Children

# "I Get a Charge Out of You"
## Teacher Information Sheet

**Objective:** To teach that an object with a static electric charge acts like a magnet

**Problem:** What will happen to a charged balloon when you move your hand in front of it?

Rubbing a balloon on your hair causes the balloon to become negatively charged. You are left with a positive charge. When you move your hand in front of the balloon you will see the strong attraction between the positive charge and the negative charge.

**Materials Needed:** (*Indicates student worksheet answers)

1. Student Scientific Method sheet
2. Individual Student Predictor
3. Classroom graph

  * 4. Balloon
  * 5. String
  * 6. Tape

## Teaching Procedure:

1. Show students materials to be used in the experiment and state the problem.
2. Pass out individual student predictors and method sheet. Students mark their hypothesis.
3. Chart all student predictions on a class graph. Ask volunteers to explain the reasons for their predictions.
4. Discuss the graph with the class focusing on mathematical concepts.
5. Conduct the experiment. (See "Procedure" on the Scientific Method sheet.)
6. Discuss results as explained in the objective.
7. Have the class complete the student Scientific Method sheet.

## Try this for fun:

Try to create the negative charge by rubbing the balloon on someone's shirt sleeve. Stick it on the wall, make a student's hair stand on end, etc.

## Example of a classroom graph:

Make a butcher paper graph. Plain tag may be used for a simple pictograph.

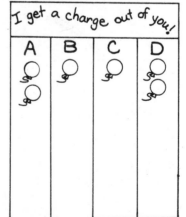

Name: _____

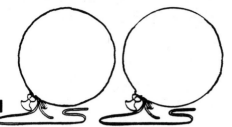

## Scientific Method
## I Get a Charge Out of You

**Problem:** What will happen to a charged balloon when you move your hand in front of it?

**Collect Materials:**

1. _____

2. _____

3. _____

**Hypothesis:** The charged balloon will _____.

        A. pop
        B. move away from your hand
        C. do nothing
        D. move toward your hand

**Procedure:** Inflate a balloon. Tie a string to it, and tape it to a table. Rub the balloon on your head to charge it. Hold your hand near the balloon, but don't touch. Watch what happens.

**Conclusion:** The charged balloon _____

_____.

Draw a picture of our experiment.

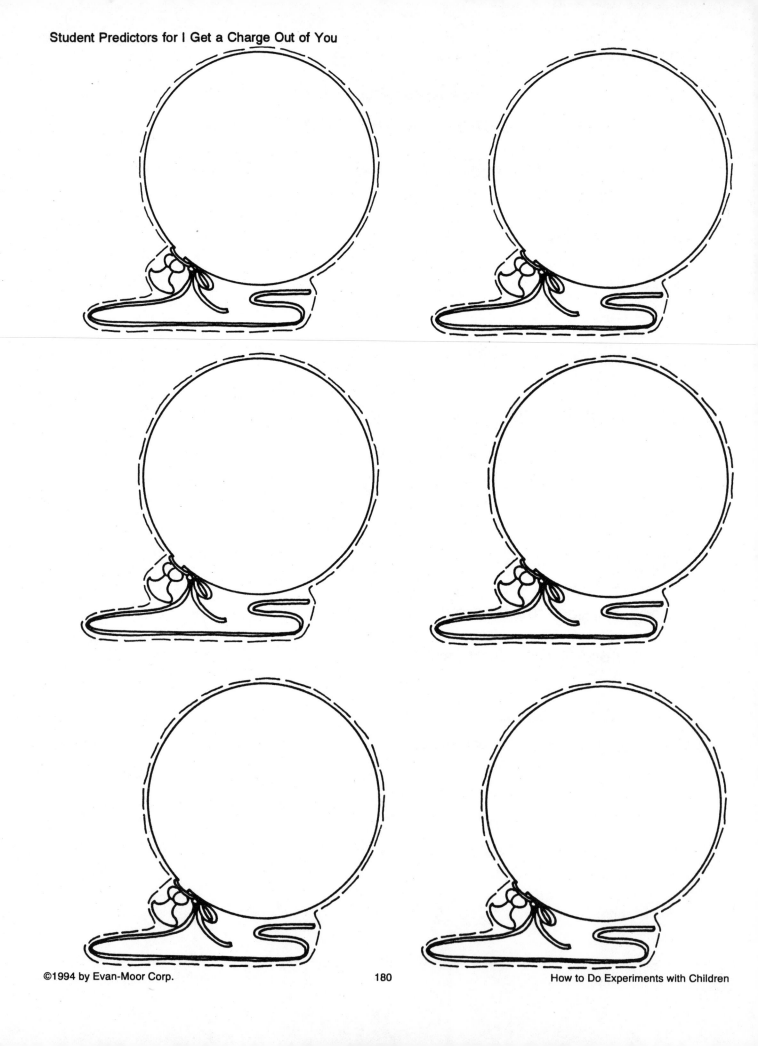

How to Do Experiments with Children

**Note:** This is fun to do the last week of school. This experiment should be demonstrated by the teacher. Y~~ou~~ want to do it outside since the cork pops vigorously and the bottle moves.

# All Gassed Up and Ready to Go.
## Teacher Information Sheet

**Objective:** To teach that for every action there is an equal and opposite reaction

**Problem:** What will happen to the bottle when the pressure of gas pops the cork off?

A basic law of motion (inertia) is that for every action there is an equal and opposite reaction. In this experiment, the action is the cork popping off and the reaction is the bottle being pushed in the opposite direction. It takes a while for the cork to pop off. Be patient and stand back!

**Materials Needed:** (*Indicates student worksheet answers)

1. Student Scientific Method sheet
2. Individual Student Predictor
3. Classroom graph

*4. Cork
*5. Bottle
*6. Baking Soda

*7. Paper towel
*8. Two pencils
*9. Vinegar

## Teaching Procedure:

1. Show students materials to be used in the experiment and state the problem.
2. Pass out individual student predictors and method sheet. Students mark their hypothesis.
3. Chart all student predictions on a class graph. Ask volunteers to explain the reasons for their predictions.
4. Discuss the graph with the class focusing on mathematical concepts.
5. Conduct the experiment. (See "Procedure" on the Scientific Method sheet.)
6. Discuss results as explained in the objective.
7. Have the class complete the student Scientific Method sheet.

## Try this for fun:

Wrap the baking powder in tissue, which disolves faster, to speed up the reaction.

## Example of a classroom graph:

Fold a piece of butcher paper in half, and sketch the outline. Cut it out. Plain tag may be used for a simple pictograph.

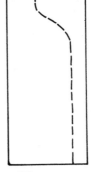

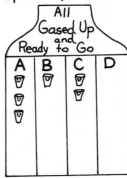

Name: _____

# Scientific Method
## All Gassed Up and Ready to Go

**Problem:** What will happen to the bottle when the pressure of gas pops the cork off?

**Collect Materials:**

1. _____    4. _____

2. _____    5. _____

3. _____    6. _____

7. _____

**Hypothesis:** The bottle will _____ .

      A. shoot in the opposite direction of the cork
      B. remain motionless
      C. spin around on its end
      D. break

**Procedure:** Pour 1/2 cup of water and 1/2 cup of vinegar into a bottle. Put a teaspoon of baking soda inside a 4" x 4" (10 X 10 cm) piece of paper towel. Roll up the towel and twist the ends shut. Drop this roll into the bottle and put the cork on tightly. Now put the bottle on its side on top of 2 pencils.

**Conclusion:** The bottle _____

_____

Draw a picture of our experiment:

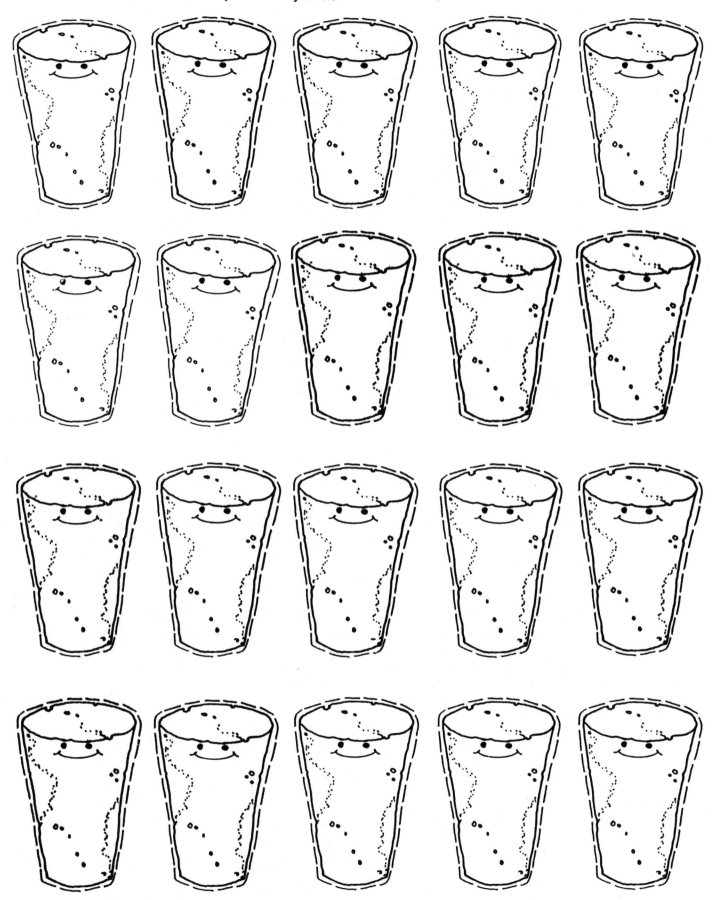

How to Do Experiments with Children

# Balloon Jets
## Teacher Information Sheet

**Objective:** To teach that all other elements being equal, the greater the amount of available fuel, the farther the balloon will move

**Problem:** Which balloon will travel the farthest?

All of the ballons in this experiment are trying to force air through the same-size openings. The air rushing out of the balloon pushes it in the opposite direction. In the same way, the hot gases rushing out of a rocket or jet push them in the opposite direction. The largest balloon (the one containing the most "fuel") will move the greatest distance down the string.

**Materials Needed:** (* Indicates student worksheet answers)

1. Student Scientific Method sheet
2. Individual Student Predictor
3. Classroom graph
*4. String
*5. Tape
*6. Three identical ballons
*7. Straw

**Teaching Procedure:**

1. Show students materials to be used in the experiment and state the problem.
2. Pass out individual student predictors and method sheet. Students mark their hypothesis.
3. Chart all student predictions on a class graph. Ask volunteers to explain the reasons for their predictions.
4. Discuss the graph with the class focusing on mathematical concepts.
5. Conduct the experiment. (See "Procedure" on the Scientific Method sheet.)
6. Discuss results as explained in the objective.
7. Have the class complete the student Scientific Method sheet.

**Try this for fun:**

Try different shaped balloons.

**Example of a classroom graph:**

Plain tag can be used for a simple pictograph if desired.

| start | Balloon Jets | finish |
|---|---|---|
| A | | |
| B | | |
| C | | |
| D | | |

Name: _____

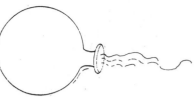

# Scientific Method
# Balloon Jets

**Problem:** Which balloon will travel the farthest?

**Collect Materials:**

1. _____     3. _____

2. _____     4. _____

**Hypothesis:** The _____ balloon traveled the farthest.

      A. large
      B. medium
      C. small
      D. It's a tie.

**Procedure:** Stretch three equal lengths of string across the room. Blow up the balloons. (Blow up one so it is large, one small, and one in between.) Hold the balloons so the air will not escape until you are ready. Attach a piece of drinking straw with tape to each balloon. Thread one string through each straw. At the signal, let all the balloons go.

**Conclusion:** The _____ balloon traveled the farthest

because _____

Draw a picture of our experiment:

How to Do Experiments with Children

# Card Sharks

## Teacher Information Sheet

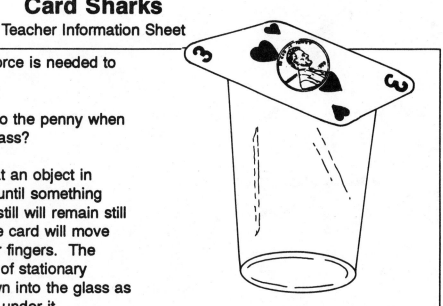

**Objective:** To teach that a force is needed to overcome inertia

**Problem:** What will happen to the penny when the card is snapped off the glass?

The basic rule of inertia is that an object in motion will continue to move until something stops it and an object that is still will remain still until something moves it. The card will move because you snap it with your fingers. The penny will not move because of stationary inertia. Gravity will pull it down into the glass as soon as the card is no longer under it.

**Materials Needed:** (*Indicates student worksheet answers)

1. Student Scientific Method sheet
2. Individual Student Predictor
3. Classroom graph

* 4. Playing card
* 5. Penny
* 6. Glass

**Teaching Procedure:**

1. Show students materials to be used in the experiment and state the problem.
2. Pass out individual student predictors and method sheet. Students mark their hypothesis.
3. Chart all student predictions on a class graph. Ask volunteers to explain the reasons for their predictions.
4. Discuss the graph with the class focusing on mathematical concepts.
5. Conduct the experiment. (See "Procedure" on the Scientific Method sheet.)
6. Discuss results as explained in the objective.
7. Have the class complete the student Scientific Method sheet.

**Try this for fun:**

Put the glass on its side with the penny inside. Move the glass quickly across the table and stop it suddenly. What happened to the penny this time?

**Example of a classroom graph:**

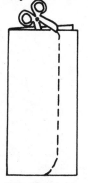
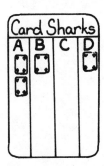

Fold a piece of butcher paper in half and sketch the outline. Cut it out. Plain tag may be used for a simple pictograph.

 How to Do Experiments with Children

Name: _____

## Scientific Method
## Card Sharks

**Problem:** What will happen to the penny when the card is snapped off the glass?

**Collect Materials:**

1. _____

2. _____

3. _____

**Hypothesis:** The penny will _____ .

        A. stick with the card
        B. drop to the floor
        C. drop in the glass
        D. change into a nickel

**Procedure:** Cover a glass with a card. Put a penny in the center of the card. Now snap the card with your finger so that it flies off the top of the glass. What happens to the penny!

**Conclusion:** The penny _____

_____

Draw a picture of our experiment:

How to Do Experiments with Children

# Fast Cash
## Teacher Information Sheet

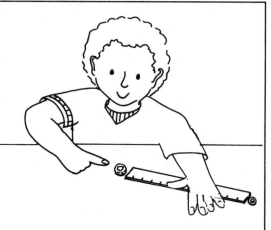

**Objective:** To teach that energy can be transferred from one object to other

**Problem:** What will happen to a dime set at the end of a ruler when the opposite end of the ruler is hit by a sliding quarter?

The quarter striking the end of the ruler (held in place) produces a force which travels through the ruler and gives the dime a push. Thus the energy in the quarter is transferred to the dime.

**Materials Needed:** (* Indicates student worksheet answers)

1. Student Scientific Method sheet
2. Individual Student Predictor
3. Classroom graph

*4. Dime
*5. Quarter
*6. Ruler

**Teaching Procedure:**

1. Show students materials to be used in the experiment and state the problem.
2. Pass out individual student predictors and method sheet. Students mark their hypothesis.
3. Chart all student predictions on a class graph. Ask volunteers to explain the reasons for their predictions.
4. Discuss the graph with the class focusing on mathematical concepts.
5. Conduct the experiment. (See "Procedure" on the Scientific Method sheet.)
6. Discuss results as explained in the objective.
7. Have the class complete the student Scientific Method sheet.

**Try this for fun:**

Try different coins. A large coin transfers more energy, making a smaller coin move faster. A small coin has less energy causing a large coin to move much more slowly.

**Example of a classroom graph:**

Fold a piece of butcher paper in half, and sketch the outline. Cut it out. Plain tag can be used for a simple pictograph.

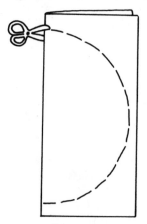
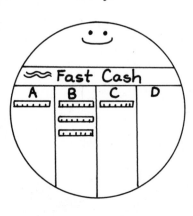

Name: _____

# Scientific Method
## Fast Cash

**Problem:** What will happen to a dime set at the end of a ruler when the opposite end of the ruler is hit by a sliding quarter?

**Collect Materials:**

1. _____     3. _____

2. _____

**Hypothesis:** The dime will _____.

        A. move under the ruler
        B. jump into the air
        C. slide away from the ruler
        D. stay where it is

**Procedure:** Place a ruler on the table and put a small coin (dime) against one end. Slide a large coin (quarter) along the tabletop so that it strikes the other end of the ruler. Be sure to hold the ruler steady.

**Conclusion:** The dime _____

_____

Draw a picture of our experiment:

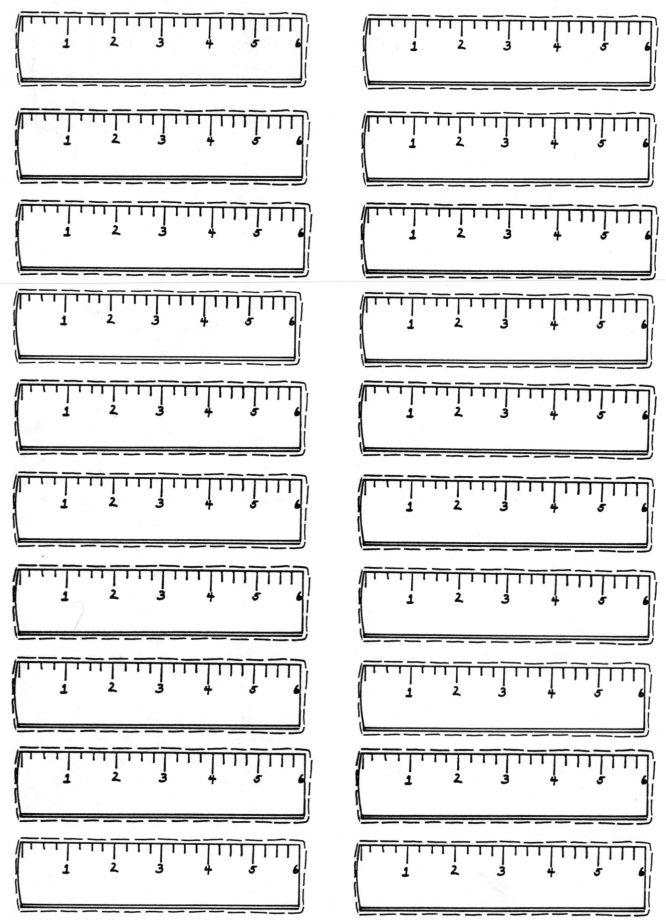

How to Do Experiments with Children

# Quick Trick

## Teacher Information Sheet

**Objective:** To teach that a force is needed to overcome inertia

**Problem:** What will happen to the bottle placed on wax paper when the paper is quickly pulled away?

The bottle sitting on the waxed paper will not move because of inertia. An object at rest will remain so until something moves it.

**Materials Needed:** (* Indicates student worksheet answers)

1. Student Scientific Method sheet
2. Individual Student Predictor
3. Classroom graph

*4. Wax paper
*5. Bottle

### Teaching Procedure:

1. Show students materials to be used in the experiment and state the problem.
2. Pass out individual student predictors and method sheet. Students mark their hypothesis.
3. Chart all student predictions on a class graph. Ask volunteers to explain the reasons for their predictions.
4. Discuss the graph with the class focusing on mathematical concepts.
5. Conduct the experiment. (See "Procedure" on the Scientific Method sheet.)
6. Discuss results as explained in the objective.
7. Have the class complete the student Scientific Method sheet.

### Try this for fun:

Try different sized bottles and different kinds of paper.

### Example of a classroom graph:

Plain tag can be used for a simple pictograph.

Name: _____

## Scientific Method
## Quick Trick

**Problem:** What will happen to the bottle placed on wax paper when the paper is quickly pulled away?

**Collect Materials:**

1. _____

2. _____

**Hypothesis:** The bottle will _____ .

        A. ride along with the paper
        B. tip over frontward
        C. remain in the same place
        D. tip over backward

**Procedure:** Place a bottle on a strip of wax paper. Pull the paper away from under the bottle with a quick motion. Watch out!

**Conclusion:** The bottle will _____

_____

Draw a picture of our experiment:

How to Do Experiments with Children

# Presto Paper
## Teacher Information Sheet

**Objective:** To teach that water molecules are attracted to one another in a magnetic fashion

**Problem:** What will happen to the wet end of an accordion-folded paper when it is held over a bowl of water?

Molecules of water have both a positive and a negative side. They attract one another like a magnet and are strong enough to pull the wet end of the paper into the water. The folding makes the paper move more easily. Use construction paper.

**Materials Needed:** (* Indicates student worksheet answers)

| | |
|---|---|
| 1. Student Scientific Method Sheet | * 4. Paper |
| 2. Individual Student Predictor | * 5. Bowl |
| 3. Classroom graph | * 6. Water |

## Teaching Procedure:

1. Show students materials to be used in the experiment and state the problem.
2. Pass out individual student predictors and method sheet. Students mark their hypothesis.
3. Chart all student predictions on a class graph. Ask volunteers to explain the reasons for their predictions.
4. Discuss the graph with the class focusing on mathematical concepts.
5. Conduct the experiment. (See "Procedure" on the Scientific Method sheet.)
6. Discuss results as explained in the objective.
7. Have the class complete the student Scientific Method sheet.

**Try this for fun:**

Try using different weights of paper.

**Example of a classroom graph:**

Plain tag may be used for a simple pictograph.

Name: _____

## Scientific Method
## Presto Paper

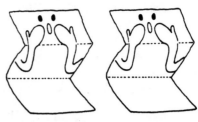

**Problem:** What will happen to the wet end of an accordion-folded paper when it is held over a bowl of water?

**Collect Materials:**

1. _____

2. _____

3. _____

**Hypothesis:** The paper will _____ .

        A. plunge into the water
        B. pull up from the water
        C. stay the same
        D. start to dissolve

**Procedure:** Fold a strip of paper like an accordion; wet one end and hold it above the water. Watch out!

**Conclusion:** The wet end _____

_____

Draw a picture of our experiment:

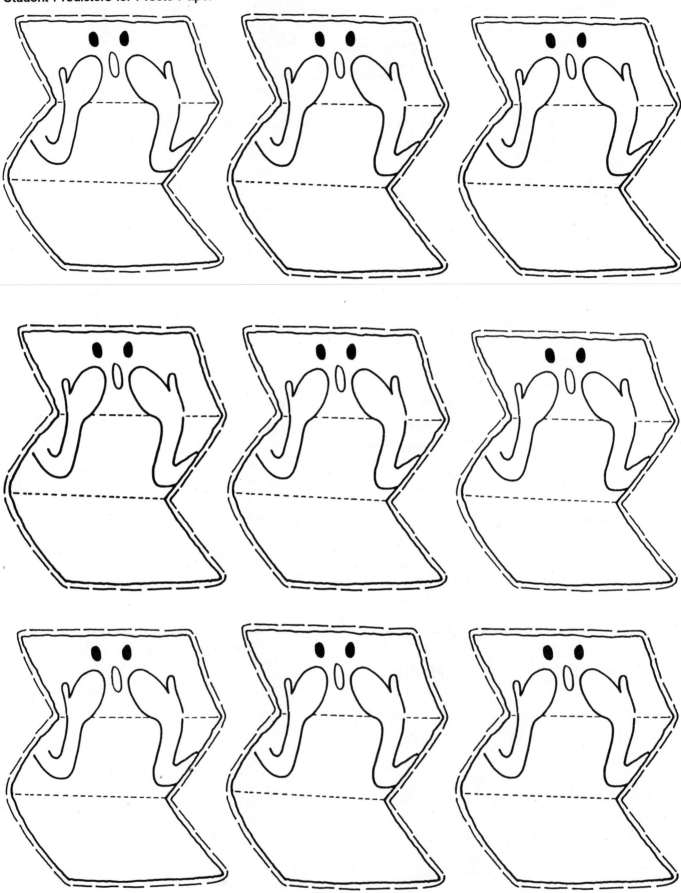

How to Do Experiments with Children

# Celery Surprise

Teacher Information Sheet

**Objective:** To teach the principle of capillary action

**Problem:** What will happen to a stalk of celery when it is placed in a glass of colored water?

Children will be able to see how water travels up the stalk of celery to the leaves. It takes about an hour for the colored water to travel up the stalk. After cutting off the end, one can see the tubes the colored water travels through to reach the leaves. The water will move up the stalk more easily if you cut .5 cm off the end of the celery to expose the phloem tubes.

**Materials Needed:** (*Indicates student worksheet answers)

1. Student Scientific Method sheet
2. Individual Student Predictor
3. Classroom graph
* 4. Water
* 5. Food coloring
* 6. Celery
* 7. Glass

## Teaching Procedure:

1. Show students materials to be used in the experiment and state the problem.
2. Pass out individual student predictors and method sheet. Students mark their hypothesis.
3. Chart all student predictions on a class graph. Ask volunteers to explain the reasons for their predictions.
4. Discuss the graph with the class focusing on mathematical concepts.
5. Conduct the experiment. (See "Procedure" on the Scientific Method sheet.)
6. Discuss results as explained in the objective.
7. Have the class complete the student Scientific Method sheet.

## Try this for fun:

Try different colors of water for seasonal activities. Try warm water instead of cold water. Warm water is absorbed faster than cold water. Re-do the experiment using flowers such as white carnations.

## Example of a classroom graph:

Fold a piece of butcher paper in half and sketch the outline. Cut it out. Plain tag can be used for a simple pictograph.

Name: _____

## Scientific Method
## Celery Surprise

**Problem:** What will happen to a stalk of celery when it is placed in a glass of colored water?

**Collect Materials:**

1. _____  3. _____

2. _____  4. _____

**Hypothesis:** The celery will_____.

        A. wilt
        B. grow more leaves
        C. expand and burst
        D. change color

**Procedure:** Fill a glass with water and add food color. Cut the bottom off a stalk of celery and place it in the water. Wait an hour. Look at the celery. What do you see?

**Conclusion:** The celery _____

_____

Draw a picture of our experiment:

How to Do Experiments with Children

# Water Works

## Teacher Information Sheet

**Objective:** To teach that surface tension is a strong, elastic bond.

**Problem:** What will happen to the drop of water when it is pulled along a maze by a toothpick?

Water is made up of many tiny molecules. These molecules stick together to form a strong, elastic bond on the surface of the water. As long as the tension does not break, water will remain as a drop. Let the children experiment with a toothpick and the drop of water on the maze. They should be able to pull it along the trail.

**Materials Needed:** (* Indicates student worksheet answers)

1. Student Scientific Method Sheet
2. Individual Student Predictor
3. Classroom graph
* 4. Toothpick
* 5. Waxed paper
* 6. Maze (page 205)
* 7. Drop of water

**Teaching Procedure:**

1. Show students materials to be used in the experiment and state the problem.
2. Pass out individual student predictors and method sheet. Students mark their hypothesis.
3. Chart all student predictions on a class graph. Ask volunteers to explain the reasons for their predictions.
4. Discuss the graph with the class focusing on mathematical concepts.
5. Conduct the experiment. (See "Procedure" on the Scientific Method sheet.)
6. Discuss results as explained in the objective.
7. Have the class complete the student Scientific Method sheet.

**Try this for fun:**

See how far the drop can be stretched before it breaks apart. Children can measure lengths to see who stretches it the farthest. Touch the drop of water with a "water disrupter" (dishwashing soap) and watch the drop of water flatten out.

**Example of a classroom graph:**

Make a chart on butcher paper as shown.

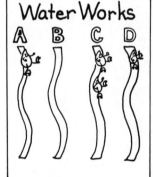

Name: _____

## Scientific Method
## Water Works

**Problem:** What will happens to the drop of water when it is pulled along a maze by a toothpick?

**Collect Materials:**

1. _____    3. _____

2. _____    4. _____

**Hypothesis:** The drop of water will _____.

        A. be absorbed into the paper
        B. stay as a drop and follow the maze
        C. do nothing
        D. spread apart

**Procedure:** Place a piece of wax paper over the maze. Make a drop of water at "start" and try to drag it with a toothpick along the trail. Watch what happens!

**Conclusion:** The water _____

_____

Draw a picture of our experiment.

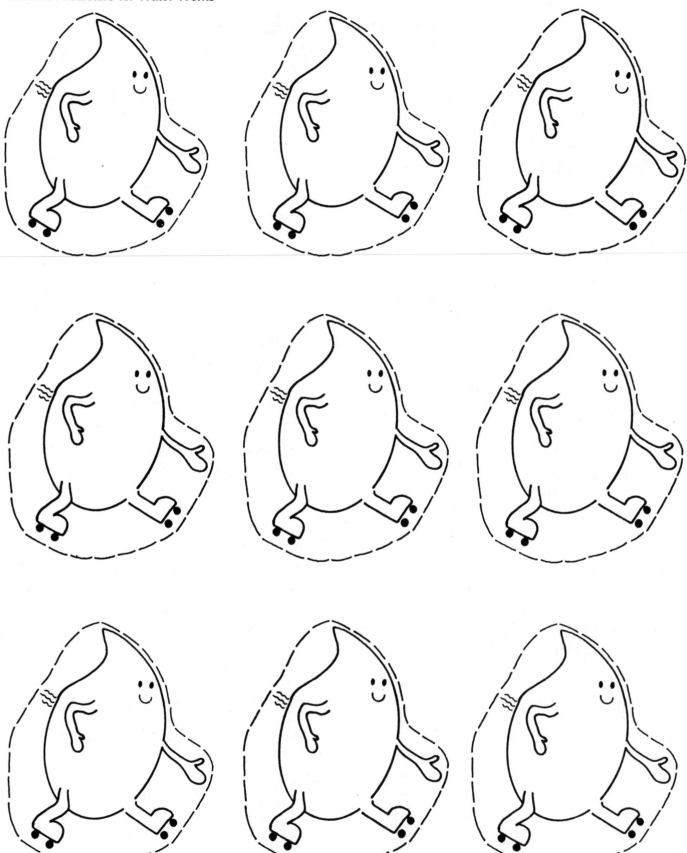

How to Do Experiments with Children

**Note:** Reproduce this form for each child or cooperative-learning group.

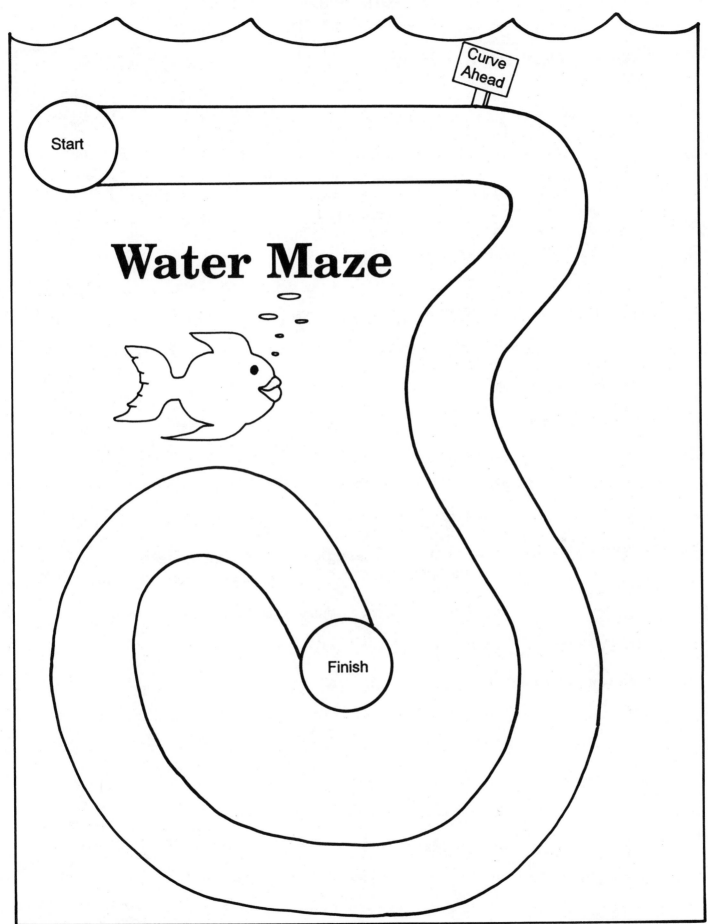

Curve
Ahead

Start

# Water Maze

Finish

How to Do Experiments with Children

# Paper Play
## Teacher Information Sheet

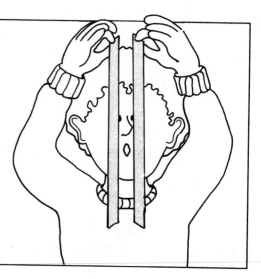

**Objective:** To teach that air moves from an area of high pressure to an area of low pressure

**Problem:** What will happen to two long strips of paper when you blow air between them?

Blowing between the two strips of paper creates a partial vacuum as moving air has a lower pressure. Therefore, the pressure on the outside of the two strips which is greater pushes the strips together to fill the area of lower pressure. Use strips of construction paper approximately 1 1/2" x 18" (4 X 46 cm).

**Materials Needed:** (* Indicates student worksheet answers)

1. Student Scientific Method Sheet
2. Individual Student Predictor
3. Classroom graph

   * 4. Two strips of paper

**Teaching Procedure:**

1. Show students materials to be used in the experiment and state the problem.
2. Pass out individual student predictors and method sheet. Students mark their hypothesis.
3. Chart all student predictions on a class graph. Ask volunteers to explain the reasons for their predictions.
4. Discuss the graph with the class focusing on mathematical concepts.
5. Conduct the experiment. (See "Procedure" on the Scientific Method sheet.)
6. Discuss results as explained in the objective.
7. Have the class complete the student Scientific Method sheet.

**Try this for fun:**

Try different lengths and different weights of paper. Balloons may be substitute for paper.

**Example of a classroom graph:**

Make a butcher paper graph as shown.

Name: _____

## Scientific Method
## Paper Play

**Problem:** What will happen to two long strips of paper when you blow air between them?

**Collect Materials:**

1. _____

**Hypothesis:** The strips of paper will _____ .

        A. fly apart
        B. come together
        C. rip to pieces
        D. make a whistling sound

**Procedure:** Hold the two strips of paper apart as you dangle them in front of your mouth. Blow between them and watch carefully.

**Conclusion:** The papers will _____

_____

Draw a picture of our experiment:

How to Do Experiments with Children

# Welcome Back
## Teacher Information Sheet

**Objective:** To teach that the movement of air over the rotors creates the area of low air pressure needed to keep a helicopter aloft

**Problem:** How can you make the paper teacher spin?

The arms of the paper teacher act like rotor blades on a helicopter. The movement of air past the teacher's arms provides lift at a speed that's enough to slow her descent and lets her float softly to the ground. To make the teacher spin, one arm is bent forward and the other backward. A paper clip on her feet provides the correct amount of weight to make her spin.

**Materials Needed:** (* Indicates student worksheet answers)

1. Student Scientific Method sheet
2. Individual Student Predictor
3. Classroom graph

*4. Teacher pattern on page 212
*5. Paper clip

## Teaching Procedure:

1. Show students materials to be used in the experiment and state the problem.
2. Pass out individual student predictors and method sheet. Students mark their hypothesis.
3. Chart all student predictions on a class graph. Ask volunteers to explain the reasons for their predictions.
4. Discuss the graph with the class focusing on mathematical concepts.
5. Conduct the experiment. (See "Procedure" on the Scientific Method sheet.)
6. Discuss results as explained in the objective.
7. Have the class complete the student Scientific Method sheet.

## Try this for fun:

Try different shapes for various holidays.

## Example of a classroom graph:

Fold a piece of butcher paper in half, and sketch the outline. Cut it out. Plain tag can be used for a simple pictograph.

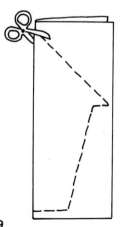

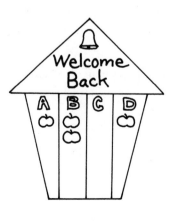

Name: _____

# Scientific Method
# Welcome Back

for Teacher

**Problem:** How can you make the paper teacher spin?

**Collect Materials:**

1. _____

2. _____

**Hypothesis:** The teacher will spin when _____ .

       A. she is dropped with a paper clip on her feet
       B. she is dropped with both arms bent forward
       C. she is dropped with a paper clip on her feet and
          one arm bent forward and one arm bent back
       D. she is dropped with both arms over her head

**Procedure:** Try all of the above choices and see which one works!

**Conclusion:** The teacher spun gracefully down when _____

_____

Draw a picture of our experiment:

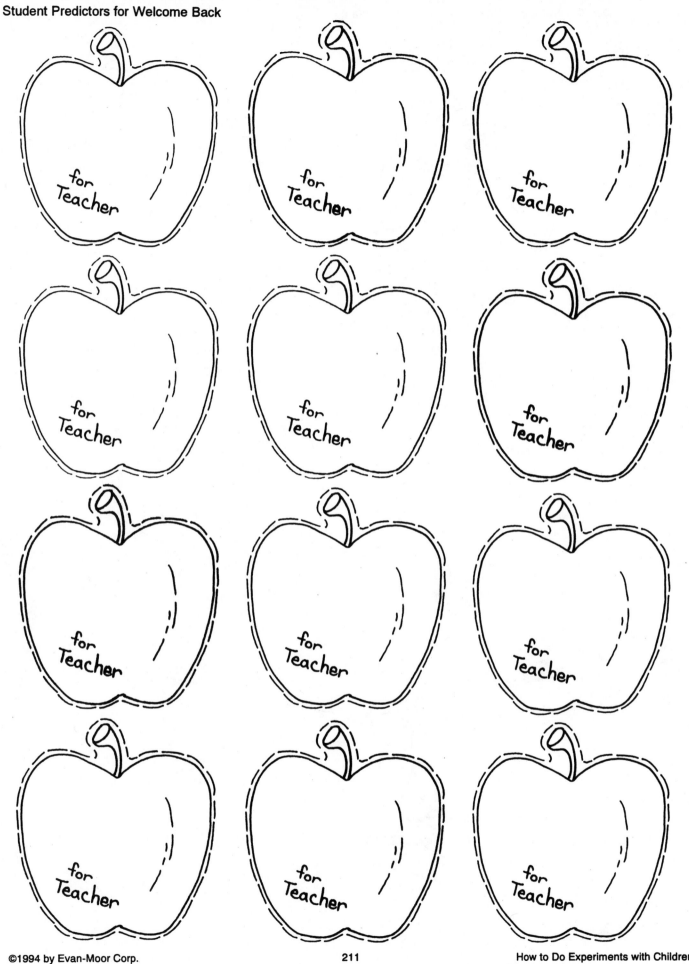

How to Do Experiments with Children

212

# Grade A Experiment
Teacher Information Sheet

**Objective:** To teach that the ability of an object to withstand pressure is affected by its shape

**Problem:** What will happen to the egg when you squeeze it with one hand as hard as you can?

An egg shell is very strong because it is in the shape of an oval. An oval is one of the strongest shapes in the world because it spreads a force equally over the entire surface. *Make sure you hold the egg in the palm of your hand. No fingers please. Also, don't wear a ring. It creates a point of pressure and you can end up with a messy hand.*

**Materials Needed:** (* Indicates student worksheet answers)

1. Student Scientific Method sheet
2. Individual Student Predictor
3. Classroom graph
   *4. Egg
   *5. Your hand

**Teaching Procedure:**

1. Show students materials to be used in the experiment and state the problem.
2. Pass out individual student predictors and method sheet. Students mark their hypothesis.
3. Chart all student predictions on a class graph. Ask volunteers to explain the reasons for their predictions.
4. Discuss the graph with the class focusing on mathematical concepts.
5. Conduct the experiment. (See "Procedure" on the Scientific Method sheet.)
6. Discuss results as explained in the objective.
7. Have the class complete the student Scientific Method sheet.

**Try this for fun:**

Try different types of eggs (such as duck or quail eggs).

**Example of a classroom graph:**

Fold a piece of butcher paper in half, and sketch the outline. Cut it out! Plain tag can be used for a simple pictograph.

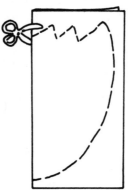
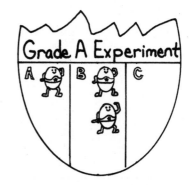

Name: _____

# Scientific Method
# Grade A Experiment

**Problem:** What will happen to the egg when you squeeze it with one hand as hard as you can?

**Collect Materials:**

1. _____

2. _____

**Hypothesis:** The egg will _____ .

        A. break
        B. crack
        C. not change

**Procedure:** Hold an egg in one hand and squeeze as hard as you can. Stand back!

**Conclusion:** The egg _____

_____

Draw a picture of our experiment:

How to Do Experiments with Children

# Can You Rock and Roll?
## Teacher Information Sheet

**Objective:** To teach that an object is pulled most strongly by gravity at its center of balance

**Problem:** What will happen to a can when a lump of clay is stuck inside the rim and it is placed on an incline?

A small coffee can works well for this experiment. Stick clay near the rim on the inside of the can. Make an incline by raising a large book with a chalkboard eraser. Now place the coffee can half way up the book with the clay at the 11:00 position. Release the can and it will roll up the "hill" because gravity is pulling the clay straight down toward the upper end of the incline.

**Materials Needed:** (* Indicates student worksheet answers)

1. Student Scientific Method sheet
2. Individual Student Predictor
3. Classroom graph

\* 4. Coffee can
\* 5. Clay
\* 6. Books

**Teaching Procedure:**

1. Show students materials to be used in the experiment and state the problem.
2. Pass out individual student predictors and method sheet. Students mark their hypothesis.
3. Chart all student predictions on a class graph. Ask volunteers to explain the reasons for their predictions.
4. Discuss the graph with the class focusing on mathematical concepts.
5. Conduct the experiment. (See "Procedure" on the Scientific Method sheet.)
6. Discuss results as explained in the objective.
7. Have the class complete the student Scientific Method sheet.

**Try this for fun:**

Try different amounts of clay and sticking it in different locations on the inside of the can.

**Example of a classroom graph:**

Plain tag may be used for a simple pictograph.

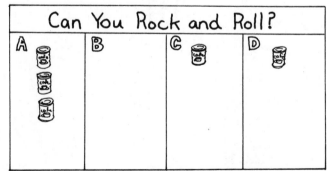

Name: _____

## Scientific Method
## Can You Rock and Roll?

**Problem:** What will happen to a can when a lump of clay is stuck inside the rim and it is placed on an incline?

**Collect Materials:**

1. _____

2. _____

3. _____

**Hypothesis:** The can will _____ .

        A. roll down the incline
        B. rock back and forth
        C. not move
        D. roll up the incline

**Procedure:** Stick a lump of clay inside the rim of a metal can. Set the can on an incline made of books. Make sure the clay is at the top of the can. Place the lid on the can. Turn it loose!

**Conclusion:** The can _____

_____

Draw a picture of our experiment:

How to Do Experiments with Children

# To the Point
## Teacher Information Sheet

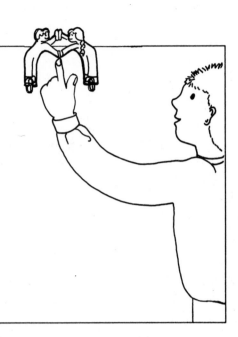

**Objective:** To teach that an object can be balanced at the point where its weight is evenly distributed

**Problem:** What will happen to the cardboard shape when it is balanced on the end of a finger?

Use tag or cardboard to make your shape. Because the paper clips add weight and the ends are long and curved, it makes the shape bottom-heavy (lowers the center of gravity). This low center of gravity keeps the shape from tipping over. (You may want to attach a penny to each end with paper clips to increase the mass below the balance point. Sometimes just the paper clip's weight is not enough.)

**Materials Needed:** (* Indicates student worksheet answers)

1. Student Scientific Method sheet
2. Individual Student Predictor
3. Classroom graph

*4. Shape (run one for each student) (page 222)
*5. Paper clip
*6. Your finger

**Teaching Procedure:**

1. Show students materials to be used in the experiment and state the problem.
2. Pass out individual student predictors and method sheet. Students mark their hypothesis.
3. Chart all student predictions on a class graph. Ask volunteers to explain the reasons for their predictions.
4. Discuss the graph with the class focusing on mathematical concepts.
5. Conduct the experiment. (See "Procedure" on the Scientific Method sheet.)
6. Discuss results as explained in the objective.
7. Have the class complete the student Scientific Method sheet.

**Try this for fun:**

Balance the shape on a pencil or even on your nose. When balancing it on your finger, try to push it over. It will pop up again when you let it go.

**Example of a classroom graph:**

Plain tag can be used for a simple pictograph.

Name: _____

## Scientific Method
## To the Point

**Problem:** What will happen to the cardboard shape when it is balanced on the end of a finger?

**Collect Materials:**

1. _____

2. _____

3. _____

**Hypothesis:** The shape will _____ .

      A. fall forward
      B. fall backward
      C. remain upright
      D. spin around

**Procedure:** Cut out the cardboard shape and tape a paper clip to each end. Balance it on your finger and let go. Try to balance it on a pencil or even your nose!

**Conclusion:** The cardboard shape _____

_____

Draw a picture of our experiment:

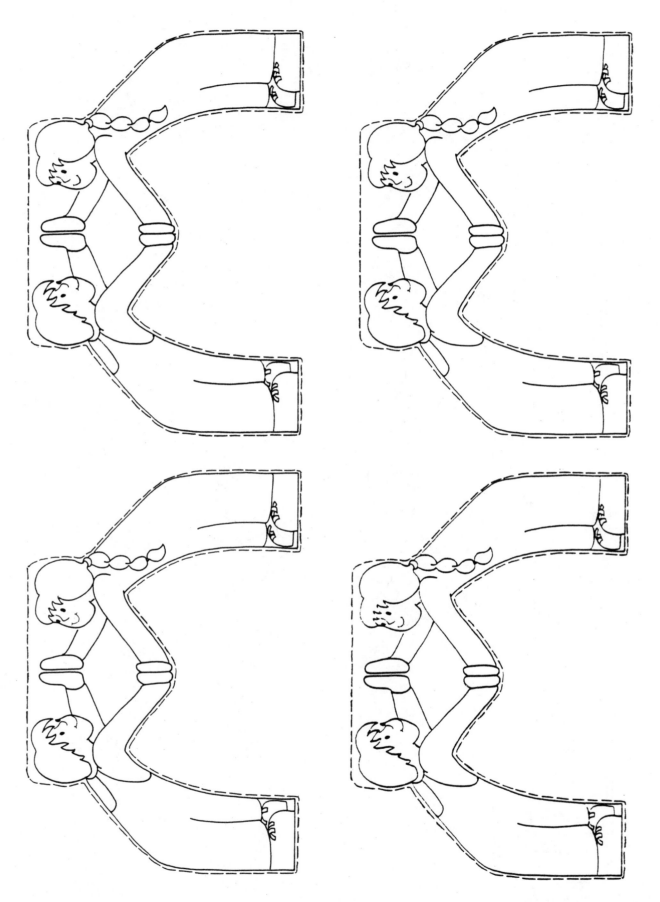

How to Do Experiments with Children

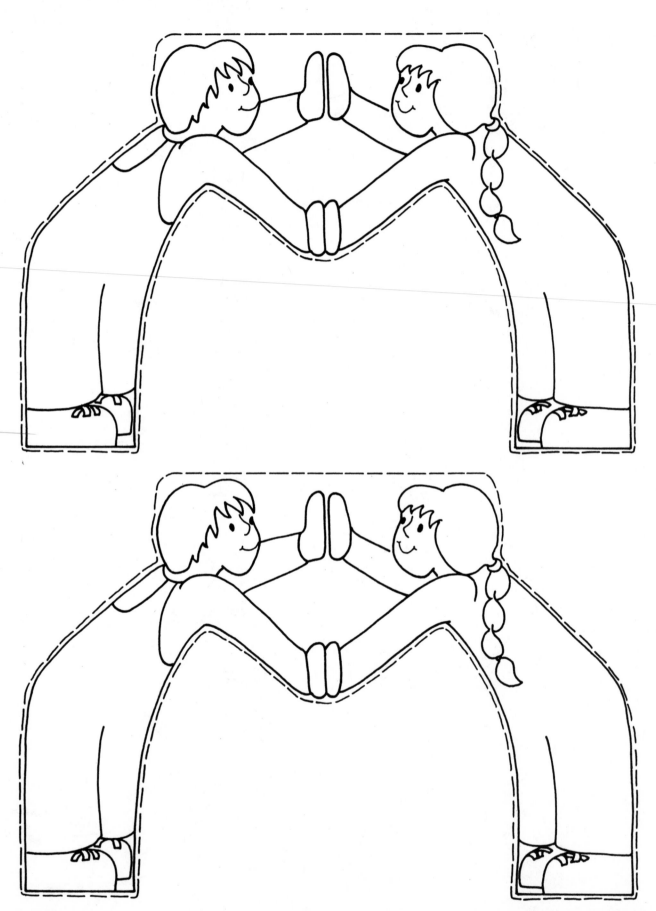

How to Do Experiments with Children

# ○ Science ○

_____
date

Dear Parents,

Our class will be doing a series of experiments in class to explore different scientific properties. The goal of these experiments is to acquaint students with many of the branches of science in an exciting and thought-provoking manner. Each of the experiments follows the scientific method, uses proper terminology, and encourages higher level thinking skills.

Your child will be bringing home a "Scientific Method" sheet for each experiment after we have completed it in class. You can take part in your child's learning by encouraging him/her to explain the purpose of the experiment, the steps followed, and the results.

Your child may wish to repeat an experiment at home. We have discussed which experiments are safe to do at home by themselves and which ones need adult supervision. I have also stressed that he/she must always check with you before doing <u>any</u> experiment.

Thank you for participating in the excitement of discovery with your child.

Sincerely,

©1994 by Evan-Moor Corp.                223                How to Do Experiments with Children

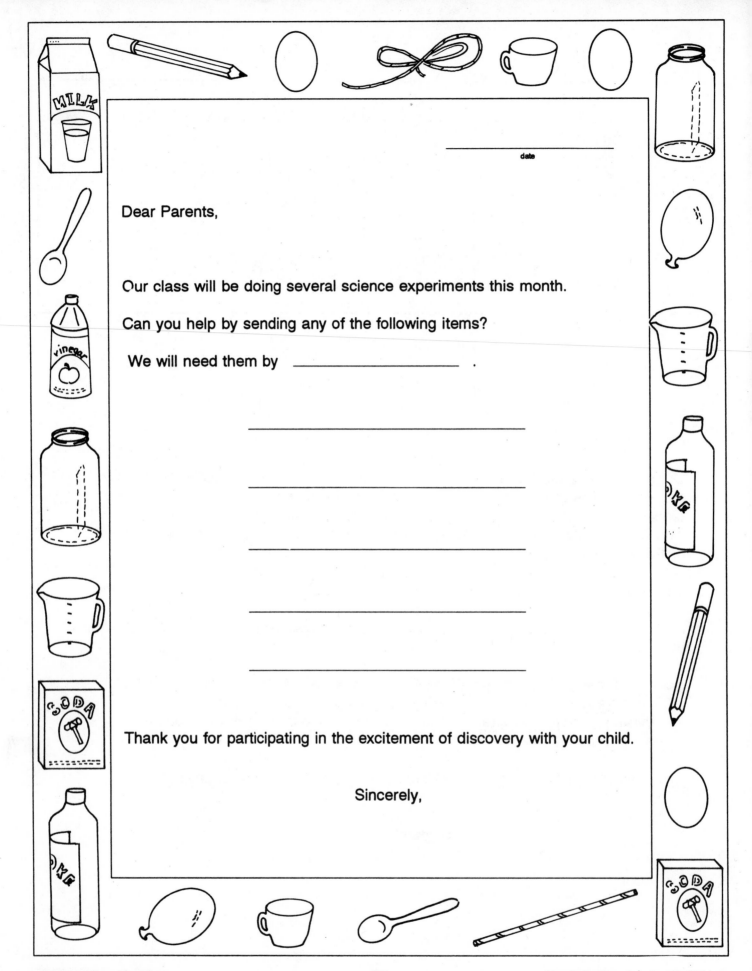

_____
date

Dear Parents,

Our class will be doing several science experiments this month.

Can you help by sending any of the following items?

We will need them by _____ .

_____

_____

_____

_____

Thank you for participating in the excitement of discovery with your child.

Sincerely,

How to Do Experiments with Children